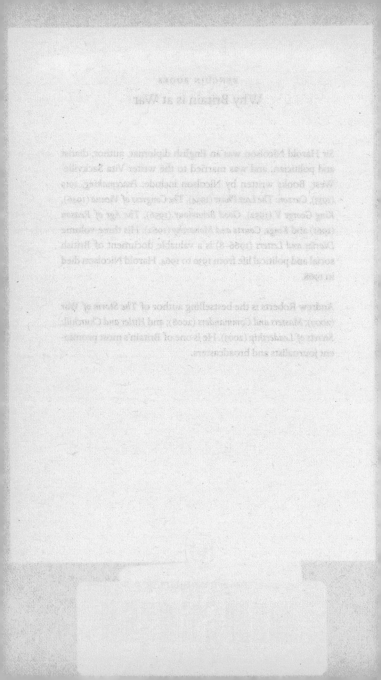

PENGUIN BOOKS

Why Britain is at War

Sir Harold Nicolson was an English diplomat, author, diarist and politician, and was married to the writer Vita Sackville-West. Books written by Nicolson include: Peacemaking, 1919 (1933); Curzon: The Last Phase (1934); The Congress of Vienna (1946); King George V (1952); Good Behaviour (1955); The Age of Reason (1961); and Kings, Courts and Monarchy (1962). His three-volume Diaries and Letters (1966–8) is a valuable document of British social and political life from 1930 to 1964. Harold Nicolson died in 1968.

Andrew Roberts is the bestselling author of The Storm of War (2009); Masters and Commanders (2008) and Hitler and Churchill: Secrets of Leadership (2003). He is one of Britain's most prominent journalists and broadcasters.

Why Britain is at War

BY

HAROLD NICOLSON

With a new introduction by Andrew Roberts

PENGUIN BOOKS

PENGUIN BOOKS

Published by the Penguin Group
Penguin Books Ltd, 80 Strand, London WC2R ORL, England
Penguin Group (USA) Inc., 375 Hudson Street, New York, New York 10014, USA
Penguin Group (Canada), 90 Eglinton Avenue East, Suite 700, Toronto, Ontario,
Canada M4P 2Y3 (a division of Pearson Penguin Canada Inc.)
Penguin Ireland, 25 St Stephen's Green, Dublin 2, Ireland
(a division of Penguin Books Ltd)
Penguin Group (Australia), 250 Camberwell Road, Camberwell, Victoria 3124, Australia
(a division of Pearson Australia Group Pty Ltd)
Penguin Books India Pvt Ltd, 11 Community Centre, Panchsheel Park,
New Delhi – 110 017, India
Penguin Group (NZ), 67 Apollo Drive, Rosedale, North Shore 0632, New Zealand
(a division of Pearson New Zealand Ltd)
Penguin Books (South Africa) (Pty) Ltd, 24 Sturdee Avenue, Rosebank, Johannesburg 2196,
South Africa

Penguin Books Ltd, Registered Offices: 80 Strand, London WC2R ORL, England

www.penguin.com

First published as a 'Penguin Special' in Penguin Books 1939
Reissued in this edition 2010

I

Introduction copyright © Andrew Roberts, 2010

Printed in England by Clays Ltd, St Ives plc

ISBN: 978-0-141-04896-3

www.greenpenguin.co.uk

Introduction

Sir Harold Nicolson (1886–1968) was a diplomat, author and politician who, for all his calm, civilized and rational exterior, was prey to profound passions. *Why Britain is at War*, a Penguin Special written on the outbreak of the Second World War, which soon became a bestseller, is a passionate and brilliantly sustained polemic against Nazism, but also against the appeasement of Hitler, against both of which Nicolson had bravely stood out during the 1930s. Equally passionate were his superbly written journals, which, in my view, constitute the finest British political diaries of the twentieth century. His homosexual passions, and the turbulent lesbian love affairs of his wife, the writer Vita Sackville-West, are well recounted in their son Nigel's 1973 book *Portrait of a Marriage*.

Born in Tehran, the third son of Sir Arthur Nicolson (the 11th baronet and later 1st Baron Carnock), Harold Nicolson attended Wellington and then Balliol College, Oxford, passing the fiendishly hard Foreign Office exams in 1909. After serving in the Madrid and Constantinople embassies he was recalled to London, and it was he who delivered Britain's declaration of war to the German embassy there. At the war's end he played a part during the Versailles Peace Conference in 1919, indeed when A. J. Balfour criticized David Lloyd George, Georges Clemenceau and President Woodrow Wilson as 'those three, all-powerful, all-ignorant, men sitting there and partitioning continents with only a child to take notes for them', Nicolson was that child. In 1920 Nicolson was appointed CMG for his efforts and promoted to First Secretary.

Postings at the League of Nations, as Counsellor at the Foreign Office and as *chargé d'affaires* at the Tehran and Berlin embassies followed, before Nicolson suddenly resigned from the service in September 1929. 'I am presented with a cactus,' he wrote of his leaving party. 'It symbolizes the end of my diplomatic career.' Some prosaic souls in the diplomatic service had failed to appreciate the books that he had written – such as the witty *Some People*, published in 1927 – and he also needed to earn more than his meagre stipend. Furthermore he wanted to see more of his beloved Vita, who had not joined him at either Tehran or Berlin.

On the left of politics, few would have predicted the next stage of his career, which was to work on the 'Londoner's Diary' column of Lord Beaverbrook's reactionary *Evening Standard* newspaper, a job he soon started to hate and which lasted only eighteen months. During that time he moved to Sissinghurst Castle in Kent, where he and his wife created one of Britain's most beautiful gardens, and he also began to keep his daily diary.

In 1931 Nicolson entered politics, standing but losing the Combined Universities seat as a candidate for Sir Oswald Mosley's New Party. He also edited the party's weekly newspaper, *Action*. He left the party the following year when its underlying fascism became evident, and before it changed its name to the British Union of

Fascists. Nicolson's utter loathing of fascism and dicta-
torship is clearly evident from Why Britain is at War. In
the 1935 general election, he was elected to parliament as
the National Labour candidate for Leicester West.

Throughout the 1930s Nicolson continued to write
assured prose in highly regarded books – such as Lord
Carnock, People and Things, Peacemaking, 1919 (about the
Versailles Conference), Curzon: The Last Phase, Helen's
Tower and Diplomacy – and after Hitler's rise to power he
resolutely opposed the appeasement policy adopted by
the National Government he had been elected to support. He was one of the few MPs in the chamber of the
House of Commons to refuse to stand up and cheer
Neville Chamberlain when he announced that he would
be flying to Munich to try to save the world from war in
late September 1938.

On 25 September 1939, less than a month after the
German invasion of Poland and Britain's declaration of
war, Allen Lane, the chairman and managing director of
Penguin, commissioned Nicolson to write a Penguin
Special of 50,000 words which would explain to the
British people why war with Germany had been un-
avoidable, and must be won. 'His deep-rooted conviction
that Hitler represented evil', recalled his son Nigel, could
now be given full rein to a mass audience. First published
on 7 November 1939, Why Britain is at War quickly sold
100,000 copies and went through three reprints by February 1940. 'There is a great deal in the book which will
annoy the Government terribly', Nicolson warned the
pro-appeasement Under-Secretary at the Foreign Office,
Rab Butler, in mid-October 1939, but two months later

Butler replied that the book 'is a work of art and perfectly correct'. Anthony Eden also told Nicolson how he was 'very much in favour of my Penguin and has bought many copies'.

The book was badly needed: Fascists, Communists and a large pacifist movement bitterly opposed the war, and between the surrender of Poland in October 1939 and Hitler's invasion of Norway and Denmark in April 1940 there was no military activity on the Western Front to distract public attention. It was being nicknamed the 'Phoney War' and the 'Bore War', and many Britons were asking the question that the superbly direct title of Nicolson's book sought to answer. His use of high irony, low sarcasm and the telling phrase – he describes Hitler as 'this lazy, feminine, unscrupulous but most remarkable man' – was ideally suited to the hour.

Inevitably Nicolson got some things wrong: it is unlikely that Hitler was ever a street-beggar, for example, and he did not allow control of events to pass to his generals. Few would today write of the Führer that 'the democratic countries have much to learn from his social experiments,' and Nicolson's proposal effectively to abolish the aeroplane after the war was naive, but overall the book is a triumph of hard-hitting prose and well-crafted propaganda. 'I face the future with sorrow,' Nicolson writes, 'with resolution, but without fear.' In teaching his fellow countrymen to adopt that attitude in 1939 and 1940, Harold Nicolson did Britain, and civilization, a great service.

When Neville Chamberlain's Tory-dominated National Government faced a vote of no confidence on

8 May 1940, over the issue of its mismanagement of the Norway campaign, Nicolson took the opportunity to vote against it, one of a group of 41 rebels to do so. (Others included Alfred Duff Cooper, Bob Boothby, Leslie Hore-Belisha, Nancy Astor, General Spears, Ronald Tree, Leo Amery and Admiral Sir Roger Keyes.) It was enough to force the Prime Minister to resign two days later, and when Winston Churchill took over as premier, Nicolson became Parliamentary Secretary at the Ministry of Information. To his intense chagrin, Nicolson held the post for only fourteen months before being sacked at the same time as his Secretary of State, Duff Cooper. The Ministry of Information was unpopular and both men were held to have failed, for all their undoubted talents beyond politics. 'I had youth and success together,' he wrote in his diary on the day of his enforced resignation, 'and now I have old age and failure.' He was 54.

A Governor of the BBC from 1941 to 1946, Nicolson's other great contribution to the war effort, besides writing *Why Britain is at War*, were his weekly 'Marginal Comment' articles in *The Spectator*, the best of which were collected and published. After unsuccessfully standing as a National candidate in the 1945 general election, he joined the Labour Party in 1947, but lost a by-election in Croydon in 1948. He devoted the rest of his life to writing, with such books as *The Congress of Vienna*, *The English Sense of Humour*, *Benjamin Constant*, *King George V*, *Good Behaviour* and *The Age of Reason*. He was sadly denied the peerage that would have allowed him to continue to contribute directly to the national debate. He died in 1968.

*

One of the most attractive personalities of his day, and showing great moral courage when his country most needed it, Harold Nicolson personified the civilization for which the free world fought. Considering that he wrote *Why Britain is at War* when Soviet Russia was still allied to Nazi Germany, and before Chamberlain's fall, it shows Themistoclean foresight as well as being an inspired, biting work of polemical eloquence. His criticisms of British politicians for not having read the 'long passages of sententious immoralising' in *Mein Kampf* were well made: even the foreign secretary Lord Halifax only perused a digest of the expurgated version of Hitler's blueprint for action.

Why Britain is at War still stands today, for all that it has been superseded by events from the Fall of France to the liberation of Auschwitz, as one of the best explanations of why Hitler had to be stopped. Its scintillating prose can be read as much for its literary as its historical merits, but it is really as a political and moral work that it bears re-reading in a modern context, especially for its certainty that: 'The virtue of human beings and not their vices in the end prevail.' Nicolson's central message transcends the war for which it was written, and speaks to us untarnished across the decades.

Andrew Roberts
January 2010
www.andrew-roberts.net

CONTENTS

CONTENTS

CHAPTER I

BRIDES IN THE BATH

At 3.15 on the afternoon of Thursday, July 1st, 1915, George Joseph Smith was convicted at the Old Bailey of the murder of Beatrice Mundy. In passing sentence Mr. Justice Scrutton informed the defendant that the jury, after a careful and patient hearing, had found him guilty of "a cold-blooded and heartless murder." He thereafter sentenced him to be hanged by the neck until he was dead. This sentence was carried out at Maidstone Gaol on the morning of August 14th.

George Smith had an excellent defence. He pointed out that he had met Bessie Mundy at Clifton, and that they had fallen in love with each other at first sight. He had married her at the local registry office under the name af Henry Williams. Miss Mundy possessed a fortune of £2,500, and on the very first day of their marriage her husband had induced her to make a will bequeathing all her worldly goods to him. They had then left together upon a honeymoon at Herne Bay. George Smith (who asserted untruly that he was particular in such matters) had insisted that their choice of lodgings must be dependent upon the lodgings possessing a wide and well-appointed bath-room. On arrival at Herne Bay, Mr. Smith (or Williams) displayed the greatest solicitude regarding the health of his bride. He assured her that she was looking very ill indeed.

She replied that she had never felt better. He insisted that they should visit the local doctor. He drew the doctor aside and informed him that his young wife had had a fit in the train. The doctor suggested the symptoms of that fit and Mr. Smith agreed that those were in fact the very symptoms which his wife had displayed. The doctor prescribed a dose of bromide. On returning to their lodgings Mr. Smith induced his wife to write a letter to her relations stating that she had been afflicted by a mysterious seizure and that the kindness of her dear husband had been beyond praise. Mr. Smith then advised her to take a hot bath. Shortly afterwards she was found dead in the bathroom. The coroner, on hearing the evidence, pronounced that she had died from drowning induced by syncope when in a bath. George Smith inherited the estate.

On the merits of that particular episode Smith possessed an almost perfect case. No shadow of suspicion rested upon him. All that he had done was to assert his rights. Encouraged by this successful speculation, he repeated the experiment. He met Miss Alice Burnham and again contracted a marriage at a registry office. He was a man of great physical charm and Miss Burnham, for her part also, fell in love with him at first sight. The same technique was applied. Miss Burnham was persuaded by her husband to insure her life and to make a will in his favour. They left on their honeymoon for Blackpool. Again he told her how ill she looked, and again he suggested that she should write to her relations informing them that she had been taken queer and how kind her husband had been. The local doctor was again called into consultation and George Smith, fortified by previous medical information, was able to explain to him exactly what symptoms his young bride had displayed. The bride herself denied that she had been conscious of any such symptoms. Mr. Smith winked at the doctor and the doctor winked at him. Obviously the poor lady had become unconscious at the moment of her seizure. They returned to their lodgings and the bride had a bath. She did not recover from that experience.

George Smith thereafter encountered Margaret Lofty. For the third time this was a case of love at first sight. The honeymoon on this occasion was spent at Highgate. Again the bride was told by her husband that she was demonstrably suffering from internal symptoms indicating a weak heart with a tendency to epilepsy. Mr. Smith advised his bride to have a bath. She also died after this experience.

A report of the inquest which was held at Highgate found its way into the newspapers. Miss Burnham's uncle happened to read this report. It seemed to him that such a repetition of misadventure was strange indeed. He drew the attention of the police to the Highgate inquest citing the analogy of his own niece's experiences at Blackpool. George Smith was arrested, tried and hanged.

It should be observed that Smith could scarcely have been convicted of the murder of Miss Mundy, had he not been so foolish as to employ exactly the same technique in his assassinations of Miss Burnham and Miss Lofty. One dead bride in a bath might well have been regarded as an unfortunate circumstance. Two dead brides in a bath might have been excused as a most regrettable coincidence. But three dead brides in a bath transcended the limits of human credulity. And George Smith was

therefore hanged owing to the fact that he had been
too stupid or too arrogant to vary his technique.

2

There are interesting comparisons to be drawn
between the case of George Joseph Smith and the
case of Adolf Hitler. Even as George Smith might
have got away with the murder of Margaret Lofty
had not his two previous brides been done to death
in an identical manner, so also might Adolf Hitler
have got away with the seizure of Danzig and the
Corridor, had he not already applied the same
technique to the destruction of Austria and Czechoslovakia. The methods adopted by each of these
two persons are not dissimilar and merit a com-
parative analysis.

George Smith's technique can be summarised as
follows:

1. Choice of intended victim and exercise of charm.

2. Every attempt made to convince the victim's
relations that his intentions were strictly honourable.

3. Marriage with victim at a registry office.

4. Victim persuaded to make a will in her husband's favour.

5. Suggestion to victim that she is looking extremely ill and is displaying marked symptoms of
epilepsy or heart-disease. Evidently grave internal
disorder.

6. Visit to local doctor to whom these symptoms
are described.

7. Letter from victim to her relations saying that
she has suffered from fainting fits and that her dear
husband has been most considerate.

8. Bath and murder.

9. Inquest withheld from the relations. Many crocodile tears.

10. Consolidation of inheritance thus acquired.

11. Preparations for next murder.

Herr Hitler's technique can be summarised as follows:

1. Choice of intended victim and exercise of charm.

2. Every attempt made to assure both the victim and her friends that his intentions are strictly honourable.

3. Treaty with, or assurances to, intended victim.

4. Preoccupation with health of intended victim. Friends and relations informed that victim is suffering from some mysterious internal disease. Symptoms of this disease manufactured artificially. German minorities organised under some Gauleiter who takes his orders from Hitler. Acts of provocation committed by these organisations. These lead to reprisals on the part of the local population or to disciplinary measures on the part of the authorities. Such measures are described as "intolerable persecution of our brothers in blood." If on the other hand the victim Government take no measures of repression the news is broadcast that they have lost control of the governmental machine and that law and order must be re-established.

5. Meanwhile foreign opinion continues to be assured of the good intentions of Herr Hitler and the justice of his cause. The ultimate purpose of destruction is concealed. Herr Hitler isolates from his real programme that part of it which will seem reasonable

and just to foreign opinion. He then puts it about that this reasonable part of his programme represents his final demands.

6. At this stage favourable terms are offered to the victim "as a basis of discussion." Yet these terms are either conveyed in a vague or tentative manner so that they are not taken seriously. Or else conveyed in the form of an ultimatum such as no independent Government can accept.

7. A press campaign is then launched against the victim.

8. Troops are massed in overwhelming force upon the frontier.

9. The pace of the negotiations is suddenly increased and the victim and her friends are informed that in view of the delicacy of the situation a settlement is not a matter of weeks or days but of hours.

10. At the last moment an attempt is made to induce the victim to send a plenipotentiary to Berlin. If he comes, he is submitted to third-degree methods and placed in the bath. If he refuses to come, then the responsibility for the ensuing bloodshed is thrown upon him. When a rupture has by this means been engineered, then the most charming terms are adduced as representing the terms which would have been offered to the bride if she had agreed to enter the bath.

11. The victim is then seized, her screams are stifled, and all compromising documents are destroyed.

12. Consolidation of inheritance thus acquired.

13. Preparations for next murder.

3

It is not only in this matter of technique that one can observe a similarity between George Joseph Smith and Adolf Hitler. The former (although an almost totally uneducated man) was convinced that he possessed literary and artistic gifts of a high order. His self-confidence was unbounded; his conceit immeasurable; his arrogance overweening. Such was his contempt for the intellectual limitations of his fellow mortals that he believed that he could defy all human morality as well as the forces of law and order. His first successes gave him such confidence in his own astuteness that he became blind even to the probabilities of chance. Yet with all his ambition, with all his greed for money, he was a mean-minded man; he haggled over the price of the coffins in which his successive brides were interred. He was an irritable man and at his trial he refused to listen tó the advice of his counsel and indulged in bursts of vituperation and rage which did much damage to his cause. To the very end he remained convinced that there had arisen some misunderstanding between himself and society and that the latter were at fault in not recognising that so great a genius stood above the rules and regulations by which lesser mortals are constrained. He went to the scaffold feeling that a great artist and a leader of men had fallen a victim to the machinations of a mediocre people. For him truth, honesty, gentleness, and moderation were little more than excuses with which lesser mortals tried to cover up their own lack of will-power. He was the perfect criminal type.

There are two points, however, at which Herr Hitler differs from George Joseph Smith. Smith was a sensualist and wished to accumulate money: Herr Hitler is an ascetic and desires only to accumulate power. And whereas Smith never committed to writing the methods by which he had planned to murder his three brides, Herr Hitler has recorded with elaborate precision the technique of his own intended stratagems.

I propose in this book to examine in some detail the three crimes committed by Herr Hitler in exercising robbery with violence against Austria, Czechoslovakia and Poland. I thereafter propose to consider the question whether such procedure concerns Great Britain; and, if so, why. But before I embark upon these three curious cases, or consider how far we ourselves need be concerned in the suppression of crime, it may be interesting to describe the origins, character and past record of Adolf Hitler and to consider that curious document, *Mein Kampf*, in which he informed the world of his own intentions. The audacity of such an avowal induced many people to assume that it was too bad to be true: the style in which it was written was such as to render it, even for expert criminologists with a sound knowledge of German, almost illegible. It was perhaps unfortunate that so few British politicians had studied *Mein Kampf* in the unexpurgated edition: the original English translation of that work omitted any passages which might cause offence to British Conservatives. Until March 15th, 1939, the British public remained convinced that Herr Hitler was, in spite of his extremely comic appearance, a "bulwark against bolshevism." They had not, I repeat, really read *Mein Kampf*.

CHAPTER II

ADOLF HITLER

ADOLF HITLER was born at Braunau in Austria on April 20th, 1889. His origins, and even his name, are obscure. Certain facts have been established. His father, for forty years, was known by the name of Alois Schicklgruber and was the illegitimate son of a miller of Döllersheim (a certain Johann Georg Hiedler), by Maria Anna Schicklgruber of Strones. Alois Schicklgruber worked as a shoemaker's apprentice and eventually obtained a small post in the Austrian customs. He was an immense man, bearing some resemblance to Marshal Hindenburg, and he married three times. It was his third wife, Klara Poelzl, who became the mother of Adolf Hitler. In honour of this third marriage Alois Schicklgruber changed his name to Hitler. We may presume that he was inspired to take this course, partly by dislike of being eternally saddled with so comic a name as Schicklgruber, and partly because the name of Klara Poelzl's mother was Johanna Hitler—a name which bore a comfortable resemblance to that of his own putative father, the miller of Döllersheim. There is reason to suppose also that the Führer's own christian name was not Adolf but Rudolf. Be that as it may, young Rudolf Schicklgruber entered upon life under the infinitely more familiar name of Adolf Hitler.

The family moved from Braunau to Linz where

Adolf was sent to school. At a very early age he
announced that he intended to become an artist, a
desire which was violently opposed by his father, who
wished him to pass his state examinations and to
enter the Austrian customs administration. Young
Hitler adopted the method of passive resistance and
refused to become educated, a refusal which proved
of much disadvantage to himself and the world in
later years. When he was twelve years old his father
died of an apoplectic fit and for five years Adolf
lounged about his mother's house, idling his time
away and refusing to complete his education. At
eighteen years of age, still convinced that he was
born to be a great artist, he travelled to Vienna and
presented himself to the Academy School of Art.
He was rejected on the grounds that "his drawings
proved unmistakably that he was not suited to be
an artist." He decided, therefore, that, as with
Michael Angelo, it was architecture and not painting
which was the true medium for his genius. At that
moment his mother died. Adolf Hitler was left alone
in the world with no education, no leaving-certificate
and only a portfolio of drawings which the Vienna
school of art had just pronounced to be bad. He
drifted back to the capital. For three years he lived
in a men's hostel in Vienna-Brigittenau, taking his
meals at a soup kitchen and finding occasional
employment as a street cleaner or as a house-painter.
There were moments when he was forced to beg
from passers-by. The hostel in which he lived
housed the dregs of the Vienna population. It was
in this drab and foulsome dormitory that Adolf
Hitler first acquired that physical repulsion for Jews
which thereafter became for him almost a patho-
logical obsession. His hatred of Jews extended to

social democrats and he was much influenced by the doctrines of Dr. Karl Leugen, the Mayor of Vienna, and a violent anti-semite. His dislike of Vienna was more than he could bear. In the spring of 1912 he left Vienna for Munich. He did not return to the Austrian capital until he entered it as a world conqueror.

At Munich Adolf Hitler was able to maintain himself by working as a builder's assistant and by occasionally selling an ugly little picture postcard of his own design. Then came the war. "To myself," he confesses, "the outbreak of war came as a redemption from the vexatious experiences of my youth. Even to this day, I am not ashamed to say that, in a transport of enthusiasm, I sank down upon my knees and thanked heaven from an overflowing heart."

2

Adolf Hitler's war-record is another mystery. As an Austrian subject his duty was to return to Linz and to present himself for service. He did, it seems, apply to the Austrian consulate in Munich. His application, for some unknown reason, was rejected. There is no evidence that as a boy he had ever undergone his military training, although it is only fair to say that he may have been exempted, owing to the lung trouble which afflicted him before he came of age. The fact remains, however, that he did not join the Austrian Army, but the German Army. He enlisted as a private in the 16th Bavarian Reserve Infantry Regiment known as the List Regiment. In November, 1914, this regiment was engaged in the Ypres sector and suffered very serious losses.

Hitler himself was not in the front line; he acted as orderly to the regimental staff. For a time he served as a mess-waiter and thereafter was employed as a despatch-runner. A legend has arisen that he was accorded the Iron Cross first class for a single-handed capture of twelve French soldiers. The regimental records contain no mention of this remarkable exploit. He was remembered only as having been unpopular with his fellow soldiers, owing to his extreme obsequiousness towards his superior officers. It is strange that he never rose above the rank of corporal, yet it may be assumed that his war-record was meretorious but none too brilliant. In October, 1916, he was slightly wounded by a piece of shrapnel. The end of the war found him in hospital suffering from gas poisoning, which had affected his eyes. Meanwhile a communist revolution had broken out in Bavaria and Munich was captured by the Soviet. On May 1st, 1919, this communist government was suppressed with extreme brutality by Colonel von Epp and his young assistant, Ernst Röhm. It was at this moment that Hitler drifted back to Munich. He had no family, he had no friends. His two sisters in Vienna did not even know whether he had survived the war. He applied to his former regiment for assistance.

The military authorities in Munich were much concerned at the time by the communist agitation which was being carried on underground among the discharged soldiers. They engaged Hitler as an *agent provocateur* and spy. His duty was to frequent the public houses in the poorer quarters of the city, to pose as being himself a left-wing agitator, and to furnish regular reports to Captain Röhm. In his autobiography he passes lightly over this unsavoury episode in his career. "I was," he writes, "detailed to the 'Commission of Inquiry into the Revolutionary Incidents' with the 22nd Infantry Regiment. This was my first more or less active political employment." He displayed great activity.

Among the many gifts possessed by this lazy, feminine, unscrupulous but most remarkable man was a genius for exploiting personal opportunities. Most spies are content to do their business and to draw their pay. Adolf Hitler exploited his job as a means of self-advancement. He began by winning the confidence, support and affection of Ernst Röhm; an affection which he retained until the day when Röhm was murdered by his orders on June 30th, 1934. He persuaded Röhm that it was possible to wean many of the workers and ex-soldiers from their communist allegiance, and to create a "national socialist" movement which would secretly further the aims and purposes of the army chiefs. Already, in addressing these tavern meetings, he had discovered in himself mysterious powers of platform oratory. He had learnt moreover that uneducated people are always much impressed if you inform them that they possess a grievance of which they had hitherto been unaware. Hitler suggested to Röhm that it would be more effective to collar the working class movement than to suppress it. He offered his services as a paid agitator on these lines. The offer was accepted.

One afternoon a junior officer pressed a slip of paper into Hitler's hand on which was written the name of Anton Drexler, founder and chairman of the "German Workers' Party", together with the address of the obscure inn at which their meetings were held. Hitler discovered the inn, attended two or three of the meetings, and eventually became a member of the Party. The total membership at that date was not more than forty. Night after night would they meet in a back room of the Steineckerbräu or the Brenessel, and Hitler would practice upon these simple people the expanding powers of his amazing oratory. It was in the course of these speeches that he developed his first formula. "You soldiers, you workmen," he screamed at them, "did not lose the war. You were stabbed in the back at the very moment of victory. You were betrayed by the Jews and the Bolsheviks. Follow me and I shall lead you to revenge and power." The effect was immediate. Until that moment they had all believed (and correctly) that the German Army had been beaten in battle by the armies of France, the United States and Great Britain. They had never thought about the stab in the back which had been dealt them by the Jews. They were profoundly grateful for this explanation of what, until then, had seemed a bitter humiliation. They gazed upon Hitler as upon some Messiah come to lead them to the promised land. Adolf Hitler also began to acquire a similar impression of his own mission.

Gradually the German Workers' Party began to expand. They decided to hold a public meeting: the audience did not number more than seven outsiders. They held a second meeting, at which the audience had swollen to eighty. They drew up a twenty-five-point programme, which was of an extreme socialist character, and they adopted the Mongolian swastika as their emblem. By February 14th, 1920, they were able to hold their first monster meeting in Munich. The military authorities purchased the Völkischer Beobachter (a small local paper then on its last legs) and presented it to Hitler. The Führer (for he was already being called by that mystic name) gradually got rid of Drexel and the other founders of the party. He assumed complete control and changed the name of his organisation to that of "The National Socialist Workers' Party," subsequently abbreviated to "Nazi." Step by step, with Röhm's assistance, he organised his S.S. and S.A. battalions, recruiting them from young hooligans who would stop at nothing in order to break up opposition meetings or secure the mastery of the streets. By the end of 1922 Adolf Hitler had become a force in Munich politics. People flocked to his meetings to witness his astonishing oratorical antics and to be assured that Germany had not really lost the war. He would engage the fourteen largest halls in Munich for a single night and dash from one meeting to the other in a powerful car. He was regarded as a curiosity, a phenomenon, an amazing agitator, an astonishing revivalist; few people took him seriously; very few people recognised in him an ominous portent.

And then came the occupation of the Ruhr.

3

IT is frequently stated that Herr Hitler was put into power by the Treaty of Versailles. It would be more accurate to say that he owed his success to Raymond Poincaré. The German people as a whole had, by the end of 1922, accepted the Peace Treaty; it was Monsieur Poincaré's insistence, against the advice of his British allies, upon occupying the Ruhr and obtaining a strangle-hold upon German industry, which drove the German public to a condition of

despairing and inflamed resentment. The whole
lower middle class saw their savings swept away in a
week and were faced with utter ruin. It was upon
a body politic utterly exhausted by inflation that the
Nazi baccillus descended with such devastating effect.

The Ruhr was occupied in January, 1923. Hitler
at once recognised his opportunity and bungled it
badly. Students of his career have always been
struck by his sudden alternations between fanatical
recklessness and physical cowardice. It was this
combination of daring and funk which almost
wrecked him for ever in the year 1923.

The first mistake occurred on May 1st. Hitler
had decided to disperse the communist May Day
celebrations in a pitched street battle. He rushed
the Munich barracks and distributed arms to his
men. The military authorities, who till then had
given him clandestine support, were enraged by this
assault. Further troops were hurried up and Hitler
and his staff were surrounded. Suddenly he lost
courage, ordered his men to surrender the arms that
they had looted, and escaped to Berchtesgaden.
No further action was taken against him. The
authorities flattered themselves that the Bohemian
corporal, the windbag of the Brenessel, had been
discredited for ever. He remained at Berchtesgaden
for a period of five months. But he was not inactive.
He placed himself in communication with Field
Marshal von Ludendorff, the ex-Commander-in-
Chief. A plot was laid to capture the Bavarian
Government and to proclaim a National Bavarian
Republic with Hitler and Ludendorff at its head.

Up to a point this plot was carried out with skill
and courage. On September 26th, 1923, the
Bavarian Government, suspecting that a revolution

was brewing, had proclaimed a state of martial law and appointed Herr von Kahr as dictator with von Lossow in command of the Bavarian Army and Colonel von Seisser at the head of the police. On November 8th Herr von Kahr was to address a large meeting in the Burgerbräukeller, a hall holding some 3,000 people in the eastern suburbs of Munich. General von Lossow and Colonel von Seisser were also to be on the platform. Hitler laid his plans with great secrecy and with the apparent connivance of the police. Kahr had just begun his speech when Hitler, who had grouped his guards around the building, burst in upon the meeting. Waving his revolver over his head he rushed towards the platform. As an eye-witness declared later "he gave the impression of a raving lunatic." His men posted machine guns at the entrances to the hall. Hitler himself, now hardly in command of his senses, leapt on to a chair, fired a pistol shot towards the ceiling, leapt down again and dashed on through the hall towards the platform, which had suddenly become deathly silent. Accompanied by his guards he jumped upon the platform, screamed out: "The National revolution has begun," and drove Kahr, von Lossow and Seisser at the point of a revolver into the adjoining ante-room. Returning to the platform, Hitler informed the terrified audience that the Bavarian Government were deposed, that the President in Berlin was deposed, that a National Government had been constituted with himself as the guiding force and with Ludendorff in command of the army. Having made this announcement he returned to the ante-room and forced Kahr, Lossow and Seisser to re-appear upon the platform with Ludendorff and shake hands all round in token of their having accepted the revolution, and of being themselves prepared to join the new government.

It was then that a hitch occurred. News was brought to Hitler that the soldiers in the barracks were trying to disarm the S.A. He left the hall in order to re-establish order. When he returned he found that Kahr, Lossow and Seisser had all escaped. Von Lossow was enraged at having been put on the spot by this insane corporal. He prepared at once for revenge. Adolf Hitler spent the remainder of the night organising his discomfited forces for an advance next day upon the centre of Munich.

At 11.0 a.m. on November 9th the march began. Ludendorff and Hitler headed the procession. They were stopped at the Isar bridge by a cordon of state police, but were able to disarm them without battle. They marched forwards until they reached the narrow street where the Loggia of the Feldherrnhalle opens upon the Odeon Platz. Here more police were drawn up. A shot was fired, and Adolf Hitler was seen to fall to the ground. A volley followed. Others fell mortally wounded beside him. General Ludendorff walked straight through the cordon of police and was arrested in the Odeon Platz. Two hours later Röhm surrendered at his headquarters. But by then the Führer was speeding in a yellow motor-car towards the Hanfstaengl villa on the Staffelsee. He had been more fortunate than his companions. Although the first to fall, he had been also the first to escape. He had run backwards while his friends were lying in the road and had leapt into a waiting car. In the rapidity of his fall he had dislocated his shoulder.

Five years afterwards Adolf Hitler staged a moving explanation of this episode. He appeared upon the platform of the Munich Lowenbräukeller, leading a boy by the hand. He explained to his audience that when the firing began he had seen this child caught in the line of fire. Sacrificing everything to his deep love for little children he had taken the child in his arms and rushed him to a place of safety. The audience were not impressed.

4

Adolf Hitler was arrested in the Hanfstaengl villa and condemned to five years imprisonment in a fortress, a sentence which was later reduced to six months. His hours at Schloss Landsberg were agreeably spent in writing *Mein Kampf* and enjoying the orchids, the laurel wreaths and the bananas with which his admirers kept him constantly supplied. He had expected that he would be received on his release as a martyr and a hero. For a few weeks he continued to be a public curiosity. After that, in the words of Konrad Heiden (from whose admirable biography of Hitler I have quoted largely in this chapter) he "ceased to be interesting." Hitler, it was assumed, had come to an end.

I can recall how in 1928, when I was temporarily in charge of our Embassy in Berlin, I received reports from Munich and elsewhere of the increasing influence of Hitler and his National Socialists. I was worried by these reports and consulted an old German friend of mine, who had for years been concerned with German politics. He replied as follows: "My dear friend, do not be misled by appearances. Were some new party in England to acquire the power which the Nazis now seem to be acquiring it might be indeed a cause for perturbation. But you do not understand that certain of our traditions strike very deep. Hitler can never become a serious menace to this country for three reasons. In the first place, he talks with a strong Bohemian accent and is therefore regarded as a foreigner. In the second place, he acted as a spy against his comrades and is therefore distrusted by the army. In the third place, he ran away during the November rising and is therefore despised by all classes of the population. A little Bohemian corporal who has been proved guilty of treachery and cowardice can never attain to a position of eminence in this country."

That, more or less, was what all serious and reliable Germans thought in 1928. Within two years from then, at the general election of 1930, the Nazi vote jumped suddenly from 800,000 to 6,500,000. Hitler became the second greatest power in the state. How is this reversal of fortune to be explained ?

From his defeat in 1923 Hitler had learnt one great lesson. He had learnt that although he possessed miraculous power over the masses, he was at a disadvantage when faced by resolute and educated men. He decided, therefore, to exploit to the uttermost his power over the people and meanwhile to conciliate the propertied classes and the army by every means at his disposal. With this in mind he dropped the twenty-five points of his revolutionary and socialist programme and decided to substitute the ballot-box for the revolver. He managed to persuade the great industrialists and the generals that he was really on their side. To the former he represented himself as the great enemy of bolshevism and social democracy. To the latter he posed as a ruthless patriot determined at any cost to restore the might and majesty of the German army. His formula was always the same: "Conceal your real intentions; conciliate your strongest opponents by pretending that you are on their side; gradually increase the strength of your position by tactical advances, each one of which is not vital enough to arouse serious opposition but the sum of which enormously add to your power; and then, at the given moment, throw down the mask and launch a mass attack upon your enemies."

Few men have better understood how to arouse the passions of the crowd. He well knew that human beings are seldom stirred to violent action by sweet reasonableness or by Christian charity. He lashed his audiences into paroxysms of rage, hatred, fear and envy. He altered the whole technique of platform oratory. In place of the table, the jug of water, the chairman and the geraniums of ordinary political meetings Hitler staged a vast emotional apparatus; a fantastic pageant. Every possible device was invented to enhance the tense drama of his sudden appearances. The audience would wait for hours in a fever of expectation, while bands increased their ardour and wild community singing brought them to the verge of hysteria. There would be a roll of drums. The lights would suddenly be extinguished and a single spot-light would be concentrated upon the doorway behind the platform. Framed in that doorway would slowly appear the lonely figure of the Führer, as some high priest emerging from the outer darkness. A wave of ecstasy would sweep over the crowd and then that strident voice would scream at them: "My fellow countrymen. Our Germany has been betrayed. . . ." Higher and higher that voice would scream out into the half-darkness. Even the coldest and most critical among his audience would find themselves affected by the surrounding orgy of emotion. I have been assured by travellers who have witnessed voodoo ceremonies and witch-dances in the Congo or the Carribbean that such ceremonies have an effect even upon the calmest nerves.

Herr Hitler, during those years, did not rely solely upon his unrivalled genius for arousing herd hysteria. He also provided himself, cautiously but rapidly, with a private army. He summoned to his side his old crony, Ernst Röhm, who after the fiasco of 1923 had gone off to Bolivia as a military instructor. By 1931 Röhm had provided him with an organised army of S.S. and S.A. men to the number of 600,000. The time had come to strike. On May 30th, 1932, Brüning fell, and with him the liberties of Germany.

It should be noticed that Hitler was assisted during those years between 1923 and 1933 by outside events. In the earlier years of his campaign his movement made little progress since conditions in Germany had improved. The Locarno treaties had done much to restore Germany's self-respect and she now found herself as an equal partner among the Great Powers. American money poured into the country and the housing and status of the working classes were being hourly improved. It seemed as if, under the beloved ægis of Marshal Hindenburg, the Weimar Republic might, after all, create a contented and peaceful nation. For five years Hitler's doctrine of hatred and revolution failed to make progress. The 1928 elections proved a defeat for the Nazi party. And then came the slump of 1929. Almost in a single day the Americans ceased pouring money into Germany and asked for their money back. Financial panic seized the whole country. Unemployment increased by leaps and bounds. The dread of a second inflation and the ruin of the bourgeoisie struck terror in every heart. The communist organisations increased in number and confidence. Hitler's second great opportunity had arrived. He seized that opportunity.

It is not necessary to trace the final steps by which, after the fall of Brüning, Hitler was able to trick Papen and Hindenburg and to seize the supreme power for himself. The device of the Reichstag fire, the sweeping victory which the ensuing panic gave him, are already sufficiently familiar. The tryanny which he thereafter imposed upon the German people, the rubber truncheons and the concentration camps, are well known. The massacres of June 30th, 1934, when Hitler rid himself of Röhm and other inconvenient friends, are not lightly to be forgotten. And his final destruction of the Jews will for long live in all our memories.

I have thought it useful, none the less, to give this account of the rise of Hitler since it illustrates both his weakness and his strength. His strength is evident; he is the greatest demagogue that the world has ever seen. His weaknesses have not always been sufficiently understood by the British people or their rulers. They can be summarised as follows:

1. Although able with consummate skill to arouse and exploit the baser passions of human nature, he is totally unable to recognise, still less to understand, that it is the virtues of human beings and not their vices which in the end prevail.

2. Although reckless and capable of feats of hysterical daring, his nerves are apt to give way at the supreme moment.

3. Although capable of inflaming the masses, he finds himself at a disadvantage when faced by strong and intelligent people.

4. Although a master of intrigue and stratagem, he is apt suddenly to lose self-confidence when faced by a simple negative.

5. Although immensely shrewd and cunning, and although possessed of a genius for exploiting any favourable opportunity, he has not the stability, the training or the force of intelligence to deal continuously with a complicated situation. He runs out of petrol.

6. Although galvanic, he is brittle.

It would be foolish to underestimate Herr Hitler or to describe as a small man one who has mastered so vast an opportunity. It would be equally foolish to overestimate the quality of his genius or to imagine that it is powerful enough to control the immense forces which he has unleashed. Many of those who listened recently to the Führer's broadcast speech from Danzig were surprised to detect in it a note of disappointment, even of mortification. It was not the voice of a triumphant conqueror, it was the voice of a broken man. And why? Because the control of events had passed from his hands into those of his generals. The star of his destiny had dimmed; the levers of power had been given into other hands; something had happened to the flaming legend of Adolf Hitler, " the greatest German there had ever been "; he felt himself to be a civilian; he felt himself again to be a corporal, a mess-waiter; he felt himself to have become once again Rudolf, son of Alois Schicklgruber, of Braunau on the Inn.

CHAPTER III

" MEIN KAMPF "

IT is possible that the preceding chapter may have suggested to some readers that I do not myself care for Herr Hitler, and that my interpretation of his actions and motives may be prejudiced. I have tried to render my account as objective as possible. I have paid my tribute to his curious genius, even as I am prepared to recognise and praise his institution of the classless state. The democratic countries have much to learn from his social experiments, and in that area of leadership I believe him to be imaginative, forceful and perhaps even sincere. The object of this book is not, however, to examine the value of Herr Hitler's treatment of the labour problem; it is to explain the reasons why friendly and peaceloving nations such as Great Britain and France should now be at war with Germany. We never wanted war; we loathe war from the depths of our souls; we have no enmity against the German people; we do not desire to extend our Empire or to destroy a commercial rival. Why, therefore, are we now at war? The answer to that question can be given in two words: "Adolf Hitler."

It thus becomes of extreme importance in any explanation of this lamentable occurrence, to define what the Hitler phenomenon really is. In the preceding chapter I have described it in terms of action. In the present chapter I propose to describe it in terms of thought. He has himself provided us with rich material for such a description. His cynicism, his ambition and his lack of all human scruple have been set out for us in his own autobiography, *Mein Kampf*.

The apologists of Adolf Hitler are apt to contend that it is unfair to judge the prophet by his own Koran. They point out that the book was largely composed in 1923, when Hitler was languishing among the orchids of his fortress prison, and when the soldiers of Raymond Poincaré were still in occupation of the Ruhr. They point out also that the more intolerable portions of *Mein Kampf* must be ascribed to Herr Hitler's lack of experience and lack of education, and that the book is little more than the excited recriminations of a tortured adolescent. Yet Hitler was not a boy when he wrote his reminiscences; he was a man of nearly thirty-five. Moreover, although foreign editions of *Mein Kampf* have been severely expurgated, the original German edition has remained intact, and is imposed upon the German public as the almost obligatory bible of their race. "We National Socialists," said Marshal Goering in a speech at Breslau in 1935, "know only one fundamental document. It is called *Mein Kampf*. Nothing else is official. There is no fundamental document other than this mighty work." And in the last place, the programme which Herr Hitler set before himself in this mighty work, the standards and principles which he there laid down, have been carried out and followed (until quite recently), in every single particular. There can be no justification whatsoever for contending that the historian is not correct in regarding Hitler's auto-biography as the central piece of evidence, as the major exhibit, in the case against him.

Even from the literary point of view the book is strange. It is turgid and ill constructed; there are endless repetitions and an almost total absence of any sense of proportion. Long passages of sententious immoralising are succeeded by pages of platform oratory. The style is always vulgar and sometimes ungrammatical. Cheap sneers alternate with screams of envy and hatred; the frequent repetition of the epithet "so-called" ("The so-called Government in Berlin," "The so-called Western Democracies") comes from the shabbiest stock-in-trade of the left-wing agitator; and the book is devoid of any depth, distinction, or even co-ordination of thought. Yet with all these faults it is a work of power. It crashes along like some river in full spate, turbid and turbulent, congested with straw and orange peel and empty beer bottles, yet expressive of fierce, destructive energy. The hatred by which it is inspired is almost demonic. The force which it generates would be impressive were it not so mean, so cunning and so shrewd. The sentences gibber at one as in some fevered dream. It is a work which inspires not admiration only, but pity and fear.

2

It is not easy to disentangle from the many repetitions and frequent contradictions of *Mein Kampf* the central thread of Hitler's philosophy. His main argument, however, is as follows:

"Man is a fighting animal and the nation is therefore a fighting unit. Any living organism which ceases to fight in the struggle for existence is doomed

B

to extinction.   A country or a race which ceases to
fight is equally doomed.   The fighting capacity of a
race depends upon its purity.   Hence the necessity
for ridding it of all foreign impurities.   The Jewish
race, owing to its universality, is of necessity pacifist
and internationalist.   Pacificism is the deadliest sin,
for pacificism means the surrender of the race in the
fight for existence.   The first duty of every country
is, therefore, to nationalise the masses; intelligence is
secondary importance; will and determination are of
higher importance.   Only brute force can ensure the
survival of the race.   Hence the necessity for
militarism.   The race must fight; a race that rests
must rust and perish.   The German race, had it been
united in time, would now be master of the world
to-day.   Is it too late for Germany to realise that
mystic function?"

Such is the main theme running through *Mein
Kampf*.   Even as a philosophy it is disturbing to
those other countries who desire only to work out
their own destiny in peace and quiet.   Hitler's racial
and power theories are not very original; they have
formed for years the material for many German
publicists; what renders *Mein Kampf* so instructive a
work is the analysis which Hitler makes of the
methods by which such world domination can be
accomplished.

He begins by a detailed consideration of the means
by which a leader should obtain supreme control
over his own people.   He takes it as his axiom that
the masses possess an essentially feminine character,
and are to be governed by emotion rather than by
thought.   The average individual does not really
care for liberty; he feels uncertain and abandoned if

he is asked to make decisions for himself; what the people really like is to submit themselves "to some dominating force, to some fanatical one-sidedness." The effect of the spoken word upon the masses is immensely greater than the written word. The popular leader must therefore concentrate upon mass meetings in which he seeks to arouse the passions of his audience. For that purpose he "must make repeated assaults upon the feelings of the least intelligent among his audience and has the actual duty to be both intolerant and untruthful." He must at the same time support himself by inspiring physical terror. The secret of any policy, whether internal or external, lies in the attack. It is not sufficient merely to stir the emotions; fear must also be inspired. "The masses," he writes, "do not come to realise that they are being terrorised and that their personal liberty is being taken from them. All that they observe is reckless power and brutality to which in the end they always succumb." "Terror," he writes again, "when applied in the shops, in the factories, in meeting places or at mass demonstrations will always prove successful." "When two conceptions or ideas," he continues, "come into conflict it is force which, if applied with sufficient ruthlessness and obstinacy, decides the issue." Can one conceive of any deeper treachery to the working class? Hitler is a natural spy.

Having established force as the final arbiter in all human affairs, Herr Hitler passes to a consideration of persuasion. He insists that all propaganda should be uniform. "If once," he writes, "a propagandist allows even the slightest glimmer of right to be seen upon the other side, he is raising doubt in the mind of the masses. The masses are not able to decide where justice ends and injustice begins. There must be no gradations, only positive and negative; love and hate; right and wrong; truth and lie; never the half and half." Above all, logical or intellectual considerations must be avoided; they only confuse the herd mind. "The great revolutions of this world," he writes, "were not brought about by intelligence or knowledge, but by some form of fanaticism which was able to inspire the masses and drive them forwards in a hysterical trance." Truth again is not a virtue which any great leader should respect. Again and again does Hitler lay it down that the born leader of men must be able to tell enormous lies. "It is better," he says, "to stick to an argument even when you know it not to be true than to provoke discussion by trying to improve upon it." "The masses," he writes again, "will fall victims to a big lie more readily than to a small one, for they themselves only tell small lies, being ashamed to tell big ones. Untruthfulness on a large scale does not occur to them, and they do not believe in the possibility of such amazing impudence, such scandalous falsification, on the part of others. Some part of even the most glaring lie will always remain behind, a fact which all associations of liars in this world know only too well."

So much for Hitler's views upon the character and intelligence of the masses in general. His remarks upon the German masses are even more cynical. He calls them "that great stupid flock of sheep, the patient but mutton-headed German people." He reproaches them for their love of peace, their tendency towards democracy, their readiness to be attracted by ideas of international order. He blames them for their irresponsibility, for their respect for knowledge and intelligence, and for "their lack of secrecy." By this strange phrase the Führer is, I suppose, referring to the frank kindliness which is so delightful a quality among the German working classes. He notes with approval, however, that the German people "are capable of waging wars for phantoms." How ghastly a phantom is that which he has now produced!

3

We are not, however, at war with Hitler because of his contempt for the virtues of the German people, or the masses in general. We may regret that he should have seen fit to crush all independent thought in his own country and have employed the magnificent machine of German state education for the production of a generation believing only in the harsh majesty of force. We may regret that in the twentieth century any Government can have imposed upon its fellow citizens such cruelties as Hitler has imposed upon the Jews and socialists. We may deplore that by his actions he has warped the soul of one of the finest races which humanity has produced. Yet we are not concerned in this particular quarrel; it is a quarrel between his countrymen and himself; it is to them that he will one day have to render account.

Yet we cannot help but take alert notice of the implications of the Nazi internal system. Let me quote the words of a great German exile, Dr. Thomas Mann:

"The meaning and purpose of the National

Socialist State is this alone and can be only this; to put the German people in readiness for 'the coming war' by ruthless repression, elimination, extirpation of every stirring of opposition; to make of them an instrument of war infinitely compliant, without a single critical thought, driven by a blind and fanatical ignorance. Any other meaning and purpose, any other excuse, this system cannot have; all the sacrifices of freedom, justice, human happiness can be justified only by the end: absolute fitness for war."

It is a sound principle of international relations that one country has no right to intervene in the internal affairs of another country. Yet when the system adopted by one country can be explained only by the determination to prepare for war against her neighbours, then those neighbours have every right to become alarmed. Their alarm can only be increased when one considers the definite avowals of aggressive ambitions which crowd the pages of *Mein Kampf*.

Herr Hitler begins his discussion of Germany's external policy by reviving the old theory of pan-Germanism. According to him the German people are destined by history to dominate the world. "Either," he writes, "we must become a world-power or cease to exist." "We are all of us aware," he writes again, "that in a distant future humanity will meet with problems which alone can be solved by a master people of the highest race supported by all the means and all the resources of the whole world. Had the German people only acquired the unity of the herd then the German Reich would to-day be master of the whole globe." It is evident that Herr Hitler is aware that this world mastery can only be achieved by a series of frightful wars. "Indeed," he confesses, "the greatest upheavals of history would be unthinkable had it not been for the driving force of fanatical and hysterical passions. Nothing could have been affected by the bourgeois virtues of peace and order."

Here speaks the fanatic, the nihilist, the revolutionary, the anarchist; here speaks the maniac who is prepared to bring the whole world to ruin in order to satisfy the only lust which he possesses; the lust of power.

4

It is unfortunate that so few British statesmen should have studied the original German edition of *Mein Kampf*, or have examined how far Herr Hitler was merely ranting, and how far he was determined to put his wild ideas into practice. Had they studied the Führer's early life and writings they would have realised in time that they were faced with a fanatic whose ambitions were undefinable because they were unlimited; whose successes in the past had been due to the fact that nobody really believed in time that this strange little man meant seriously what he said; who respected no law either of God or man; and whose avowed method was one of violence and trickery, coupled with that shrewdness which enabled him to make the best of every opportunity, to bide his time, and to exploit the weak sides of his opponents. Successive British cabinets, in their lethargy and optimism, preferred to believe that Germany could easily be "satisfied" when the convenient moment came. Those who warned them that they were faced by a man of the utmost ruthlessness were dismissed as alarmists. Mr. Winston Churchill again and again during those years rose in the House of Commons and begged successive cabinets to prepare the country against the oncoming typhoon. He was accused of being "deficient in judgment," of basing his view upon unofficial gossip; of taking a sentimental, nay, an academic, point of view; of wanting war.

Those British statesmen who had actually read *Mein Kampf* had read it only in the English edition, from which demure volume all "fanatical and hysterical passions" had been expunged. It is not surprising that they should have failed to notice the spirit of destruction which is its essential inspiration. They noticed only those passages which convinced them that (whatever the cranks of their own Foreign Office might say) Hitler's essential policy was "pro-British" and "anti-Russian." "Whatever happens," they thought, " the explosion will go east."

There were, it is true, certain grounds for this belief. Herr Hitler, when he wrote his book, did not believe in a Russian alliance.

"Present day Russia," he wrote, "is no ally in the struggle for liberty of the German nation. Looked at from a purely military point of view a war with Germany—Russia against the West of Europe, but more likely against the whole world, would be an overwhelming catastrophe. The struggle would be fought not on Russian but on German soil without Germany receiving any real support from Russia. The very fact of a treaty with Russia would be the signal for a new war. Its end would be the end of Germany."

This may well prove the most correct of all the Führer's prophecies. Yet our Ministers, when the Foreign Office disclosed to them their recurrent nightmare of a German-Soviet alliance, should not have dismissed this warning as an "F.O. bogey." They should have interpreted the above sentence from *Mein Kampf* in the light of Hitler's general diplomatic theory. "Every question," he wrote, "of foreign policy can only be considered from this point of view: will such a solution be of advantage for our people now or in the future, or will it cause us damage? All considerations of internal politics, or religion, or humanity, in brief every other consideration whatsoever, must be pitilessly eliminated." The Führer had no faith in collective security, in the ideals of the League of Nations, or even in pacts of mutual aggression. "An alliance," he wrote, "the aim of which does not comprise the intention of waging war, is meaningless and unreal. Nations only conclude alliances in order to fight." It should also have been noticed that when Hitler attacked bolshevism he attacked it because of its Jewish origins and connections. He never attacked Stalin.

Ignoring in this manner the essential implications of Herr Hitler's thoughts on foreign policy, the British Government attributed to his exposition of Nazi diplomacy an importance which it did not in fact possess. They failed to understand that his programme had been sketched out at a moment when France appeared to be the dominant Power in Europe and when it seemed incredible that France and Great Britain would ever allow Germany to fortify her western frontier and to become again the most potent military factor in central Europe. They based their interpretation of his foreign policy upon statements which, when he achieved power, were already out of date. They did not see that when it came to a choice between the lean goats of the Ukraine and the rich cattle of the French and British Empires, Herr Hitler would prefer the cows to the goats.

Yet when one examines the programme enunciated in *Mein Kampf*, there is much to explain the "peace in our time" school. Herr Hitler outlined his 1923 programme in definite terms; the mistake was to imagine that any such programme would be applicable to conditions as they existed in 1935. All he wanted, he said, was "soil and territory." William II had made the mistake of seeking such soil and territory overseas, an error which brought him inevitably into naval conflict with Great Britain. The Third Reich would make no such mistake. Their conquests would be continental and not oceanic. "We must," wrote Hitler, "direct our gaze towards land in the east. In seeking for the enlargement of the living space of our people in modern Europe we can only find it (in the first place) in Russia and the subject states upon her borders. . . . Above all we are not policemen charged with the duty of protecting 'poor little nations'; we are the soldiers of our own nation."

His plan was as follows. It did not seem possible in 1923 for Germany to attack her eastern neighbours without forcing France to intervene. The only hope was to wean England to the side of Germany; there were many influential people in London and even in the provinces who would collaborate in this difficult task. "To conciliate the favours of England," he wrote, "no sacrifice would be too great." Events proved that there was no need to make any sacrifice.

England was ready to concede every favour provided she were left in peace. Herr Hitler imagined in 1932 that he would have to offer England "common success, common conquests, and a common extension of power." It took him six years to realise that England did not desire success, was bored by conquests, and horrified at any prospect of the extension of her responsibilities. It took him six years to realise that Russia was the only country which could be tempted by the imperialist bait. Meanwhile, and for many years, his mind concentrated upon this idea of getting England to help him against France. He may still cherish this idea. "Such an alliance," he wrote, "would afford Germany the opportunity to make, wholly undisturbed, such preparations as would be necessary for our final settlement with France. Its advantage would be that it would not expose Germany to any sudden foreign invasion, whereas it would itself break the Entente and would thereby isolate our mortal enemy, France." "An eventual success," he added slyly, "might be that by a sudden stroke Germany could free herself from an unfavourable strategical position."

By that, of course, he meant the inability of Germany to construct a Siegfried line. He did not foresee that the French and British Governments would unite in permitting that construction.

It seems almost unbelievable that any foreign Government, possessing knowledge of Adolf Hitler's origins and previous record, having before their eyes the document in which he had confessed the unlimited scope of his ambitions, the true nature of his opportunism and the cynicism of his methods, could still have hoped that this anarchist could be satisfied by minor concessions or controlled by reasonable persuasion. Yet that, in fact, was the type of optimism in which the French and British Governments, in their anxiety to avoid inconvenient predicaments, consistently indulged. They were fortified in this escapism by the passages in *Mein Kampf* which I have just quoted. There is another passage which would, had they noticed it, have warned them of the method which the Führer was likely to adopt. It runs as follows:

"A wise victor will, if possible, always impose his claim on the defeated people stage by stage. Dealing with a people which has grown defeatist—and this is every people who has voluntarily submitted to force—he can then rely on this fact that in not one of those further acts of oppression will it seem sufficient reason to take up arms again."

It was this principle which Adolf Hitler adopted in the three main crimes which he committed against European order. He adopted it in regard to Austria and Czechoslovakia. He tried to adopt it as against Poland; but, even as Mr. George Joseph Smith, on this third occasion he went too far.

CHAPTER IV

THE SEIZURE OF THE RHINELAND

SATURDAY, MARCH 7TH, 1936

THE following argument is often raised: "But if Herr Hitler is no more than a homicidal maniac, how comes it that the great mass of the German nation regard him with religious devotion; and how comes it that he has been able to outwit all European statesmen?"

The answer to that question is as follows:

1. Herr Hitler is much more than a homicidal maniac. He is resourceful, intelligent, shrewd, secretive, cunning and possessed of terrific will-power.

2. It is questionable whether the great mass of the German people do, in fact, regard him with religious devotion. Apart from the Jews, socialists and other political opponents, most of the saner and more experienced elements in the country regard him with terror. It is from the younger generations and from the uneducated masses that he draws his support. It must be remembered also that the German people are more gullible and neurotic than other peoples. The nerves of even the most stolid nation would have cracked under the long ordeal to which the German people were exposed between 1914 and 1933; the German nation (in spite of appearances) is anything but a stolid nation.

3. The psychological factor must also be taken into account. Herr Hitler, in an almost miraculous manner, was able to identify his personal rancour with the rancour of a whole people. He had failed in his examination, they had failed to win the war; he had gone through years of poverty and oppression, their experience had been the same; he had found himself despised and rejected by his fellow countrymen; they had found themselves rejected by the nations of the earth. He had longed with flaming passion to raise himself from subservience to domination; that also was the passion which smouldered in every German heart. Let me again quote Konrad Heiden: "Hitler shaped his people with tremendous suggestive power after the pattern of his own wounded vanity, filling it with hysterically exaggerated notions of honour, power and superiority, and with all the errors and prejudices of the defeated." That is a true and subtle explanation.

4. Neither the success nor the prestige of Hitler has been as continuous as is supposed. In 1923 the Germans regarded him as a joke; in 1928 they regarded him as a comic episode which had petered out; as late as 1932 they thought him mad. To-day they may regard him as an inspired genius, a Messiah sent from heaven to give them the mastery of the world. Yet when once the magician fails in his magic, when once his "somnambulist certainty" leads him to stumbling, he will again be suspected of being a reckless and half-demented charlatan.

5. His diplomatic success, up to March 15th, 1939, was indeed phenomenal. Until then he was dealing with foreigners who persisted in believing that he was fundamentally as human as they were themselves. His concentrated will-power triumphed

over their optimism and lassitude. It was so far
more comfortable to take his plausible assurances at
their face value. Yet when he tore up the Munich
agreement on March 15th, he also tore the mask
from his face. It remains to be seen whether that
error was not the most catastrophic error ever
committed by any leader.

2

Let me resume for a moment my short narrative
of Herr Hitler's actions and career. In 1924 the
Nazi movement was regarded as dead. After four
years of intensive work Hitler was only able to win
twelve seats at the 1928 election. Then came the
slump of 1929–1930. The Nazi representation rose
to 107 seats. Unemployment continued to increase
and by 1931 the workless in Germany numbered
7,500,000. Hitler adopted a dual policy. He reassured the propertied classes and the army by
substituting for his old doctrine of "revolution" his
new doctrine of "legality." He assured the
authorities (to whom he was always slyly subservient,
gently plausible, until the moment came when he
felt strong enough to overthrow them) that he would
only act by constitutional means. Röhm's private
army of 600,000 concurrently increased its reign of
terror throughout the country. In 1932 Hitler tested
his popularity. He stood for the Presidency against
Marshal Hindenburg; it was the new vulgar Germany
defying the old dignified Germany; Hitler polled
11,000,000 votes, but the old Marshal polled
18,000,000. The Führer continued his system of
toadying the powerful and bullying the weak. The

elections of July 3rd, 1932, gave him 230 seats and rendered the Nazis the strongest single party in the State. The Führer insisted arrogantly that he should at once be made Prime Minister. Hindenburg refused. It was then that Hitler, as in 1923, began to make his mistakes.

He made three mistakes. In the first place he abandoned his pose of "legality" and massed his private army round Berlin. He spoke of a "massacre of St. Bartholomew." In the second place, he publicly insulted the aged President Hindenburg, who was the idol (and rightly) of the German people. And in the third place, he announced that "I am clearly conscious of the great tasks which Providence has assigned to me." The German people were shocked by this utterance, which seemed to them both blasphemous and mad. Hitler thereupon tried to upset Chancellor von Papen in the Reichstag. The trick miscarried. Papen had already provided himself with a decree signed by President Hindenburg dissolving the Reichstag. On November 6th, 1932, new elections were held. The Nazis lost 2,000,000 votes. Disaster seemed to be imminent. The party was deeply in debt, and at an election in Thuringia held shortly afterwards they lost half their seats. Hitler was in despair. His rocket was falling to the ground. He was rescued from ruin owing to dissension among his opponents.

Papen had been succeeded in the Chancellorship by General von Schleicher. Each of these two bid against each other for the support of the Nazi party. Schleicher, somewhat foolishly, endeavoured to induce Strasser, one of Hitler's dissident lieutenants, to revolt against the Führer. Papen was more wise. On January 4th he held a secret interview with Hitler and promised, in return for an alliance, to pay the Nazi debts. On January 30th Papen persuaded the aged President (with whom he had great personal influence) to appoint Hitler Chancellor and himself Vice-Chancellor. The President agreed. Even then Hitler was not quite certain of his position. He decided to continue on the lines of "legality" until he had obtained complete physical control over the country. What was required was, first to create panic and then to create a general election. On February 27th he set fire to the Reichstag building and proclaimed that this had been done by the communists as the signal for a general uprising. The trick worked splendidly. The whole upper and middle classes were seized with panic. At the ensuing election the Nazis were returned with an overwhelming majority. The levers of power were in the Führer's hands.

Or were they? As the months passed he became uneasy. Papen, who found that Hitler did not display that gratitude or consideration which he had counted on, made a speech at Marburg in which he sneered at the Nazi system. What was even more disturbing was that Ernst Röhm had increased his S.A. army from 600,000 to 3,500,000 men. Supposing that Röhm were to employ that army to seize supreme power for himself? Evidently a "purge" was necessary. Hitler retired to Bad Godesberg, where a former comrade of his, of the name of Dreesen, kept a hotel. Röhm had summoned a conference of S.A. leaders to Wiessee in the Bavarian highlands for June 30th. The Führer was also expected to attend. He did attend. Leaving Bad Godesberg at 2.0 a.m. by aeroplane, he landed at Munich two hours later and was met by Himmler and picked detachments of the S.S. They drove at once to Wiessee, where they discovered Röhm and his friend Heines still in bed. Heines was murdered on the spot; Röhm was taken back to Munich and shot a few hours later in the Stadelheim prison. At the same moment other planned assassinations were taking place all over Germany. The total casualties are not known. It is estimated that nearly 700 people were done to death. "June 30th, 1934," writes Konrad Heiden, "is the most sanguinary event of modern German history."

Herr Hitler did not confine his attentions to those who were associated with Ernst Röhm. It was an excellent opportunity to rid himself of his enemies as well as of his friends. Two of von Papen's secretaries were murdered in their office as a warning; the Vice-Chancellor himself barely escaped with his life. General von Schleicher and his wife were shot in their Berlin apartment. Nor did Hitler's memory of past grievances fail him for a moment. Von Kahr, who had been responsible for the 1923 failure, was now living in retirement near Munich. The body of this old gentleman of seventy-three was found lying naked in the marsh near Dachau, having been cut to pieces with hatchets.

The purge was complete.

3

Having achieved supreme power and having rid himself of all dangerous enemies or inconvenient friends, Herr Hitler settled down to the task of rendering Germany the dominant Power in Europe. It was not an easy task. Under the treaties of peace,

Germany was precluded from possessing a military air force, from increasing her standing army, from introducing conscription, and from fortifying the Rhineland. The late Captain Röhm's creation of an unofficial army of 3,500,000 men went far to solve the immediate problem of man-power. What was needed was the rapid enrolment and training of officers and N.C.O.s. It was also necessary to turn the whole unemployed population of Germany on to the night and day construction of aeroplanes and munitions. Conscription would also have to be introduced sooner or later. And, above all, the Rhineland must be occupied by strong military forces and an impregnable barrier of fortresses constructed in that demilitarised area. All this tremendous work would have to be carried out without arousing the suspicions, or provoking the intervention, of France and Great Britain. It was essential to lull the two western democracies into a sense of security during the dangerous period in which these preparations were being made.

Hitler used gentle words. It had always been considered that the danger point in Europe was the corridor and the free city of Danzig. As early as January, 1934, Herr Hitler entered into a treaty with Poland accepting the Versailles frontiers and pledging himself not to seek to disturb those frontiers for a period of ten years. In London and Paris this agreement was hailed with relief. The appeasers were entranced. Evidently, they felt, Herr Hitler is a wise and moderate statesman. But meanwhile the arms factories of Germany were throbbing night and day. Again and again did Winston Churchill and others warn the government of what was happening. Again and again were their warnings dismissed as fantastic or alarmist. Every device of the German propaganda system was employed to lull anxiety in this country. Prominent Conservatives and their wives, were invited to Berlin and assured of the pacific and pro-British feelings of the Nazi rulers. Even schoolboys were used as anæsthetics. The effect was exactly what Hitler desired. He was allowed to complete his preparations undisturbed.

The method he has adopted in gradually increasing and extending his power has always been the same. First lull your opponents into a sense of security; then suddenly seize some strategic position which, although of immense value to yourself, is not so inordinate as to provoke the peace-loving countries to military intervention; then proclaim that this is your last and only adventure, and lull, thereby the democracies to sleep again while you prepare for the next.

Thus, when in 1935 he intervened with the whole force of his propaganda machine in the Saar plebiscite, he assured France that, if he obtained the Saar (as he did obtain it) he would become for ever "satisfied." When, a few months later, he broke the existing treaties by establishing conscription throughout Germany, he was equally ready with assurances and at once opened negotiations with Great Britain for an Anglo-Nazi agreement by which he recognised the overwhelming superiority of the British Navy. Encouraged by the success of these manœuvres, and by the fact that France and Great Britain remained indifferent to his vast rearmament and to the creation of an enormous mechanised army and air force, he proceeded, early in 1936, to plot the most stupendous stroke of all.

4

It will be remembered that at the time of the Peace Conference, Marshal Foch and others had warned the statesmen of Europe that it would be impossible, after a few years had passed, to prevent the secret of even overt rearmament of Germany. The only means by which the Western Powers could guarantee their future security against a revived Germany was to maintain the military control of the Rhine frontier. "That river," Foch used to say, "will settle everything." These views were regarded by the civilian directors of the Conference as "militaristic." In their place, was substituted an elaborate scheme under which certain Rhineland areas and bridgeheads should be occupied by the Allies for varying terms of years; under which Germany would be permanently forbidden to erect fortresses, or to maintain military establishments, in the Rhineland: and under which Great Britain and the United States promised to come to France's assistance if she were ever attacked.

The latter guarantee was rejected by the United States Senate and the British Government decided (foolishly perhaps) that in these circumstances their own obligations must also lapse. Yet some sort of security pact had to be devised for this area of European danger. It was due to the wisdom of Briand, Stresemann, Austen Chamberlain and D'Abernon that a far better system was invented. Instead of forcing a solution upon Germany, as had been done in 1919, Germany was invited to enter a pact as an equal partner to a free discussion. In return for this she received great benefits, above all, the withdrawal of allied troops from German territory before the date stipulated in the Versailles Treaty. She promised on her part to observe articles 42 and 43 of that Treaty, which laid down that the Rhineland must remain permanently unfortified. The Treaties embodying this arrangement were negotiated at Locarno in October, 1925. They led to an immense improvement in the relations between Germany, Great Britain and France.

Herr Hitler's difficulty was this. In the first place, he could not say that the demilitarisation of the Rhineland was a condition imposed upon Germany by the brutal Treaty of Versailles, since Germany had, six years after Versailles, willingly accepted that condition as a free negotiator of the Locarno Treaties. In the second place, he was well aware that to fortify the Rhineland would be such a tremendous blow to European security that France and Great Britain would, as they were bound to do under the letter of the Locarno Treaties, intervene by military action. He would not, at that date, have been able to resist such intervention. He gambled, however, and against the advice of his General Staff, upon the chance that French and British opinion would not be prepared for war, and that the British public and politicians would not (*in time*) understand the true implications of what was happening. He therefore, with cunning and daring, adopted his accustomed tactics.

He first stated that he was anxious to enter into friendly discussion with France and Great Britain for some modification of the Rhineland statute, accompanying this offer by the attractive bait of an agreement to prevent aerial bombardment in war.

These negotiations were still under discussion when, on the morning of Saturday, March 7th, 1936, the German armies poured into the Rhineland. We now know that their commanders had received instructions to withdraw at the slightest sign of opposition. No opposition was offered. The British and French Governments had been taken completely by surprise.

In Berlin, on the same day, Herr Hitler denounced the Locarno Treaties on the ground that the conclusion of a pact between France and Russia had rendered them invalid. At the same time he sought to lull all anxiety by offering to the world a peace pledge lasting for twenty-five years, an air pact, and Germany's re-entry into the League of Nations. His terms were almost identical with those offered on October 6th, 1939. The British public, who had been most inconvenienced by this act of aggression, seized upon this excuse to acclaim that "all was all right really." *The Times* newspaper, with its usual optimism, reassured its readers in a leading article entitled: "A chance to rebuild." That caption was more accurate than they supposed. It was indeed an amazing chance. It was a chance for Herr Hitler to reconstruct a highly militarised state without interference on the part of the Western Powers. It was a chance for him to extend his power over Eastern Europe, to render himself by successive conquests and expansions, impervious to any blockade and therefore impervious to the might of the British navy. It was a chance to enter into close contact with Russia and to remove from Germany the danger of a war on two fronts. It was a chance to become the arbiter of the world's destinies.

I recollect with sadness the effect of the Rhineland occupation upon the House of Commons. The

opposition, although most suspicious, were delighted
by Herr Hitler's offer to re-enter the League of
Nations. The Conservatives were anxious to explain
that Herr Hitler's dramatic gesture had, in fact, been
a gesture of appeasement. "Can you really contend," they argued, "that seventeen years after the
war Germany does not possess the right to fortify
her own territory?" "Do you really mean," they
protested, "that the lives of our young men should
be sacrificed for the sake of the French militarists?"
It was useless to explain that once Hitler was secure
in the west he would mop up Austria, Czechoslovakia, Poland and Rumania. That he would then
enter into an agreement with Russia. That he would
then threaten the British Empire in alliance with
Italy. And that we, having surrendered all our outer
fortresses, should find ourselves fighting for life or
death upon the cliffs of Dover. Such arguments
were dismissed as "A dirty intrigue against the
Government." They were described as "fouling our
own nest." Such warnings were brushed aside as
"The gloomy but wholly academic forebodings of
those who possess the Foreign Office type of mind."
It was not pleasant during those weeks to be a
Cassandra exposing weakness, indicating danger, and
prophecying disaster. The statesmen and the politicians, the Knights and the Baronets, were determined
to be optimistic. And they were. Good heavens!
They were.

How delighted, during those March days of 1936,
must Herr Hitler have been! He had scored off his
own General Staff who had advised him that his
master-stroke was too dangerous to be attempted.
He had told them that the French and British public
were too stupid to understand, and too timid to act;

that their Governments, being dependent upon public opinion, would inevitably hesitate until it was too late. Without losing a man he had attained what, in 1923, had seemed to him a fortress to be attained only at the price of a terrible and uncertain war; he had obtained that " *Rückentdeckung* " that protection in the rear, which would enable him to execute his programme of expansion. The Western Democracies had been proved to be fools and cowards. He could ignore them, or almost ignore them, in the future.

Little more was heard of the famous peace offer of March 6th. The device had served its purpose; the bait had hooked its fish. When, therefore, on May 7th, His Majesty's Government enquired politely what exactly the Führer had meant by this offer, he did not even trouble to reply.

Hitler had won hands down.

CHAPTER V

THE SEIZURE OF AUSTRIA

SATURDAY, MARCH 12TH, 1938

HAVING, by this master-stroke, secured himself against the victors in the Great War, Herr Hitler felt that he had now sufficient *Lebensraum* to embark on further adventures. It had always been one of the most cherished of his dreams to incorporate Austria within the German Reich. "It stands me in good stead," he had written in *Mein Kampf*, "that Fate decided that Braunau on the Inn should be my birthplace. This little town lies on the frontier between the two German States, the re-union of which we younger ones at all events regard as our life task, to be accomplished by all means within our power." "Finally," he wrote again, "I wanted to be amongst those who had the fortune to be on the spot and play my part in the country where my heart's most burning desire was bound to be fulfilled; the union of my beloved country to the common Fatherland, the German Reich." The words of this latter sentence are, as so often in Herr Hitler's writings, ungrammatical and obscure. The sense is plain. One of his first objects on coming to power was the seizure of Austria. We may question whether this desire was inspired by any particular love for Austria; it was inspired rather by his passionate zeal for German expansion and by his anxiety to assuage his vanity which had been so wounded by failing in his school-certificate and during the unhappy days in Vienna. What a triumph if the vagrant postcard-seller of the Viennese doss-houses could return there in a fine Mercedes car and even sleep in the bed of Franz Joseph at Schönbrunn! Yet here again there were difficulties in the way.

In the first place, Article 80 of the Treaty of Versailles laid it down that "Germany acknowledges and will respect strictly the independence of Austria; she agrees that this independence shall be inalienable except with the consent of the Council of the League of Nations." In the second place, Hitler was well aware that it was a cardinal point in the policy of France, Italy and the smaller States in Central and South-Eastern Europe to prevent such incorporation by every means in their power. A premature attempt which the German Government had made in 1931 to spring a sudden Customs Union upon Europe had been met with determined resistance and had exposed those who launched that attempt to a serious humiliation. Hitler learnt from this experience that he should bide his time.

He believed, however, that he could attain his ends by organising an internal illness in Austria and by placing Vienna in the hands of the local Nazis. From the moment that he assumed the Chancellorship of the German Reich he instructed his agents to organise a Nazi party in Austria and supplied them liberally with money and arms. He was assisted in this endeavour by the internal conditions of Austria itself and by the jealousies which existed between those who should have united to defend Austrian independence against German aggression.

No country had suffered more from the war than

the former Austro-Hungarian Empire. Austria, at one time senior partner in a Dual Monarchy which embraced some 52,000,000 people, saw herself suddenly reduced to a small republic of only 6,500,000. Before the war the frontiers of the Austro-Hungarian Empire had stretched from Southern Poland to the Adriatic, from the Bohemian mountains to the borders of Rumania. Vast forests, great mountain ranges, rich mineral resources, huge belts of grain-land, ports, harbours and water-ways rendered the Empire a magnificent area of wealth and beauty. Through this vast empire flowed the Danube, and in the centre glittered the gay capital of Vienna—light-hearted, artistic, easy-going and content. The war changed all that. The city of Vienna was too large for the territory of which it was now the swollen centre. Financial collapse, economic ruin and actual starvation seemed to threaten. At the last moment Austria was rescued from death by the intervention of the League of Nations. The rescue of Austria remains one of the most brilliant achievements that the League ever accomplished. It was managed by Sir Arthur Salter.

Austria, thereafter, began to revive. The two great parties in the State were the Christian Socialists on the Right, and the Social Democrats on the left. These two parties shared between them some 80 per cent of the total Austrian vote. The remaining 20 per cent went to the Pan-Germans from whom the eventual Nazis were recruited. Had the two strictly Austrian parties not fought each other with internecine bitterness it would have been impossible for the Nazi minority to establish itself in the country. Some coalition between the right and the left ought to have been possible after Hitler's advent to power in Germany. Socialists loathed him for his fascist brutality; the Catholics detested him for his anti-religious methods. The Chancellor of the time, Engelbert Dollfuss, was a man of charm and courage who was affectionately known in many quarters as "Austria's pocket Chancellor." Although a determined supporter of Austrian independence, he failed to see that by attacking his Socialist opponents he was leaving the road open for Nazi infiltration. In February, 1934, he attempted, with unfortunate success, to disarm the Socialists, and the ruthlessness with which he executed this policy lost him much sympathy in the democratic countries. Hitler imagined that his chance had come.

The terrorism which his agents of the "Austrian Legion" had for months been conducting in Austria was intensified after the events of February. The Governments of France, Great Britain and Italy became alarmed. They issued an announcement to the effect that they took a "common view of the necessity of maintaining Austria's independence and integrity in accordance with the relevant treaties." The Italian Government went further. They concluded with Austria as with Hungary the agreements of March 17th (known as the "Rome Protocols") which, in effect, established Italy as the protector of Austrian independence. Hitler was undeterred by these pronouncements. By the beginning of July the Führer, having by that time finished off his own purge in Germany, decided that the moment had come to strike. A rising was organised for the 25th July. The Vienna broadcasting station was occupied with much bloodshed by the Nazi irregulars; risings broke out in Carinthia and Styria; and Chancellor

Dollfuss was murdered in his office by the assassins
Planetta and Holzweber.

The Austrian army remained loyal to their own
country. The rising was rapidly suppressed. Germany was prevented from intervening from across the
border by the fact that Italy mobilised divisions upon
the Brenner pass. Hitler was quick to retreat from
the false position in which he found himself. He
disclaimed any previous knowledge of the conspiracy; he recalled his Minister from Vienna on the
grounds of indiscretion and sent von Papen in his
place; he withdrew the Austrian Legion from the
Bavarian frontier; and he called off the Nazi Terror.
It was not until March, 1938, when he had finally
consumated the seizure of Austria, that he confessed
his complicity by hailing the assassins of Dollfuss as
martyrs in the cause of German nationhood.

2

After the failure of the first Nazi coup against
Austria of July, 1934, Herr Hitler decided that he
must approach his victim by more stealthy means.
He concentrated all his energy upon rendering
Germany comparatively secure from external
pressure, with the success which has been recounted
in the previous chapter. He then proceeded to woo
Italy, who was rapidly becoming estranged from the
Western Powers as a result of her Abyssinian adventure. The great obstacle to any agreement between
Italy and Germany was this very question of the
independence of Austria. Italy, it was felt at the
time, could never under any circumstances allow the
presence of a German army on the Brenner Pass or

tolerate any German threat towards her harbour at Trieste. Herr Hitler decided that for the moment it would be wise policy to allay Italy's fears. He therefore, on July 11th, 1936, concluded an agreement with Austria. The terms of this agreement, in view of subsequent events, must be recorded.

Germany recognised "the full sovereignty of the Austrian Federal State," and promised to exercise no influence, "either directly or indirectly," upon the internal affairs of Austria. Austria, on the other hand, "acknowledged herself to be a German state," but added that this would not affect the position of Austria in regard to Italy as defined by the Rome Protocols. Certain secret articles were added to this Treaty. It was agreed that Nazi organisations might be established upon Austrian territory "provided they did not seek to influence Austrian citizens by propaganda." The Austrian Government also agreed to grant an amnesty to all Nazis other than those accused of criminal offences. From then onwards the Nazi organisations in Austria rapidly increased in power. A Committee of Seven was established, the Secretary of which was Dr. Leopold Tavs. This organisation became the headquarters of the Nazi internal movement. The bride became very ill indeed.

In spite of these secret clauses (of which he may well have been unaware at the time) Signor Mussolini appears to have been completely set at ease by the German-Austrian Agreement. The Rome-Berlin axis began to function almost immediately. Only six days later, with German assistance, General Franco raised the standard of revolt in Spain and the long-drawn comedy of non-intervention on the part of Germany and Italy began.   In the autumn of that year the axis, under the name of the "Anti-Comintern Pact," took upon itself a triangular shape and included Japan. Hitler then set the stage for his second attempt upon the life of the Austrian republic. He allowed an interval of a year and a half to elapse.

British opinion also had been much comforted by the Austro-German Agreement. *The Times*, on July 13th, 1936, wrote as follows:

"Herr Hitler has brought off another stroke of policy upon which . . . he is certainly to be congratulated. The agreement with him which has been freely made by the Austrian Government cannot but help to stabilise and pacify Central Europe, improve its economic conditions, and pave the way for a permanent settlement between the two branches of the German Race."

It would appear that *The Times* had no knowledge of the secret clauses. It was these clauses which paved the way.

On January 30th, 1937, Herr Hitler reassured the world by announcing that "the period of surprises is ended." On January 26th, 1938, a second attempt was made upon the life of Austria; it failed even more ignominiously than its predecessor. On that date Dr. Tavs, Secretary to the Committee of Seven, was arrested by the Austrian Government, and the papers found in his apartment in the Tierfaltstrasse showed that a widespread rising had been planned. These papers included written instructions from Rudolf Hess to Leopold Tavs ordering him to create disorders in Austria in the first weeks of April. Herr Hess (Hitler's deputy) assured Leopold Tavs that such a large proportion of the Austrian police were secret Nazi sympathisers that he had nothing to fear. He should, therefore, seize as many public buildings as possible and create a situation which would oblige the Government of Dr. Schuschnigg to intervene to restore order. The moment the first shot was fired, German troops, who would be concentrated on the Austrian border under the excuse of manœuvres, would enter for the purpose of "preventing bloodshed."

The arrest of Dr. Tavs, and the seizure of this compromising document, upset the German plan. A further difficulty arose. General von Fritsch, the Commander-in-Chief of the German Army, bluntly informed the Führer that he would not allow the German army to be employed for such purposes.

Herr Hitler, for the moment postponed his plan. He took precautions to ensure that such a miscarriage of injustice should not occur again. On February 4th, General von Fritsch and thirteen other senior officers were dismissed from their posts and, at the same time, Baron von Neurath, who belonged to the moderate school, was succeeded as Foreign Secretary by Herr von Ribbentrop, who did not belong to the moderate school. General von Fritsch has since been murdered.

The surprises thereafter followed thick and fast.

3

On February 12th, 1938, Dr. Schuschnigg, the Austrian Chancellor, was summoned urgently to an interview with the Führer at Berchtesgaden. Papen, by that time relegated to the post of German Ambassador in Vienna, assurred him that all that was

needed to adjust the relations between Germany and
Austria was a frank and friendly conversation.   Dr.
Schuschnigg innocently left for Obersalzberg, taking
under his arm the portfolio containing the case
against Dr. Tavs.   He seems to have imagined that
Hitler would be impressed by these revelations of the
extent to which his agents had violated the Agreement of July, 1936.   On arrival at the Führer's villa
he was for long kept waiting in an anteroom on the
walls of which hung a huge map of the Austro-
German frontier.   From time to time busy staff
officers would rush into the room and move a flag an
inch or two forwards.   Dr. Schuschnigg noticed
with alarm that each flag represented a German
division and that whole army corps were being
rapidly concentrated upon his own frontier.   After
sufficient time had been allowed to Dr. Schuschnigg
thoroughly to appreciate these overwhelming and
rapid troop movements, he was admitted into the
presence of the Führer himself. .

Dr. Schuschnigg produced his papers about Dr.
Tavs.   The Führer for some minutes remained silent
gazing with vacant eyes at the ceiling.   He then
started to his feet and discharged upon Dr. Schuschnigg such a torrent of rage, of rhetoric and of vituperation as has seldom fallen from the mouth of
man.   Not only did the Führer not disclaim Dr.
Tavs, he thoroughly approved of him.   The fearful
persecutions to which the Austrian Nazis were being
subjected by Dr. Schuschnigg cried to heaven for
revenge.   How could he, Adolf Hitler, "the greatest
German that had ever lived," stand by idle when his
brothers in blood were being subjected to excrucia-
ting tortures.   The 1936 agreement had been torn
up and spat upon by Herr Schuschnigg himself.

Such a situation was unbearable. It must be put an end to now and for ever. The Austrian Chancellor must sign a document immediately agreeing to appoint Dr. Seyss-Inquart, a prominent Nazi, to such a position in the Austrian Ministry of the Interior as would place him in charge of the whole Austrian police force. The Foreign Office must at once be handed over to Dr. Guido Schmidt, another of Herr Hitler's Vienna agents. Other pro-German Ministers must be appointed to the Cabinet. Political prisoners must be released. And Nazi propaganda and organisations must be admitted within the Austrian Republic. Failing agreement within three days, the Führer would order his armies to cross the border and to "restore order" in Austria.

Dr. Schuschnigg was a brave and honourable man. He refused to sign any such document on the ground that he could not do so without submitting it to his Cabinet and to Dr. Miklas, the President of the Austrian Republic. He agreed, none the less, to give Seyss-Inquart the desired appointment. Reeling from this torrent of invective, he returned to Vienna still carrying under his arm the papers about Dr. Tavs. He was faced with an impossible situation. Almost immediately Dr. Seyss-Inquart (who on receiving his appointment had at once flown to Berlin to receive his instructions from Herr Hitler) provoked pro-Nazi demonstrations throughout Austria. There were demonstrations at Vienna, in Graz and at Linz at each of which Seyss-Inquart was present.

Again did the Nazi Government attempt to re-assure the victim and her relations. On February 18th the *Völkischer Beobachter* (Herr Hitler's official journal) published a leading article which contained the following sweet words:

"The conversations between the Führer and the Austrian Chancellor reveal a welcome relaxation of the bad feeling between the two German States, justifying the expectation that the differences which stood in the way of carrying out the July agreement have now been finally overcome. Can there be a better answer to the international press agitation against the Reich and the rumours of a Putsch in Austria than this new joint contribution to the peace of Europe?"

Dr. Schuschnigg himself appears to have shared with the international press an apprehension that a Putsch was, in fact, contemplated. On March 9th he decided to play his trump card. He announced that on the following Sunday a plebiscite would be held in order to prove that the majority of the Austrian people desired to retain their independence and refused to be incorporated in the Reich. It was known that he would obtain a majority of from 60 to 80 per cent. Herr Hitler became alarmed. On March 11th, he sent, by the hand of Seyss-Inquart who had been summoned to Berlin, an ultimatum to Dr. Schuschnigg insisting that the plebiscite should be postponed. The Austrian Chancellor replied agreeing to do so provided that the Nazis would, for their part, refrain from disturbing order. This reply did not satisfy the Führer. A second ultimatum was presented which was to expire at 7.30. In this it was demanded that Dr. Schuschnigg should resign, that Seyss-Inquart should become Chancellor in his place, that two-thirds of the seats in the Cabinet should be given to the Nazis, and that the Nazi party in Austria should be granted unrestricted freedom. At 7.30 p.m. Austrian listeners heard for the last time the voice of Dr. Schuschnigg upon the wireless. It was his farewell message. He announced that the invasion of Austria had been threatened "from this hour" unless he resigned in favour of a cabinet nominated by Germany. In order to avoid any bloodshed he had decided to resign. "I take my leave," he concluded, "with a German word and a German wish— *God Guard Austria*." Hardly had he finished, when Seyss-Inquart went to the microphone and announced delightedly that German troops had already crossed the frontier and were even then marching on Vienna. The capital was occupied next morning at seven; by six the same evening Herr Hitler made an hysterical entry into Linz, the very town in which, as a boy, he had failed to pass his school-certificate. Within a short time he was driving through the streets of Vienna in a large Mercedes car.

The loot which Hitler obtained from the murder of Austria was considerable. In the first place his reserves of man-power were increased by more than 10 per cent. In the second place he acquired valuable raw materials, such as magnesite of which Austria was one of the world's chief sources of supply. And in the third place he secured what, in the state of his finances, he needed most, namely cash and credits. It is estimated that the Nazi Government looted from Austria something like 290,000,000 marks, or nearly four times their own reserves. In addition they cancelled all foreign holdings of former Austrian nationals and thereby increased their overseas assets. Large private fortunes were made by individual Nazis by holding the Viennese

Jews up to ransom. It was a most profitable undertaking.

4

The effect of this aggression upon other countries was diverse. The Central European countries knew all too well that they themselves would be the next on the list. France, which at the moment of the crime had been without a Government, felt bewildered and insecure. Mussolini found himself in a very awkward situation. He had broken his traditional friendship with Great Britain in order to adhere to the Berlin-Rome alliance. It had been understood that one of the main conditions of this axis was the independence of Austria. Austria had been swallowed up in a single night; The German troops had, with great rapidity and less tact, occupied the Brenner posts on the very first evening. What could Mussolini say? If he confessed that he had not been consulted, then it would be obvious to all the world that he was but a sleeping partner in this unwelcome alliance. If, on the other hand, he announced that the German seizure of Austria had been carried out with his approval, then Catholic opinion, and Italian opinion generally, would be incensed. Mussolini decided that the best thing was to lie low. On that Saturday he fled to the mountains. When it came to settle up accounts he would demand from Germany, as a repayment for this overt humiliation, her support in obtaining control over the Mediterranean.

And what of opinion in Great Britain? Once again the optimists buzzed around. "Was it not natural, nay was it not right, that Germany should join with her brothers across the border?" "Surely this violation of the German-Austrian pact would throw Italy into the arms of England?" "Now that he had incorporated Austria, Hitler would surely feel satisfied." "The Austrians, in any case, were unable to manage their own country."

Such were the evasions by which British public opinion tried to escape from the inconvenient and unpleasant realisation that Hitler's Germany was out for loot. Eden, a few days before the seizure of Austria, had resigned from the Cabinet. Now was the moment to make friends with Italy. The full proportions of the German danger were still too unpleasant to realise. British public opinion shrank away into the undergrowth of optimism and excuse.

Their optimism was, to some extent, diminished when full accounts and the films of the German occupation of Vienna came through to the cinemas and the newspapers. The question arose whether, if the Austrians had, in fact, been so anxious to join with Germany, that junction need have been celebrated by so much artillery and so many tanks. Why should 1,742 people have been arrested? Sad stories came through of Nazi persecutions. The Jews of Vienna had been turned on to clean the streets. Elderly Jewish ladies, walking in the parks of Vienna, had been forced by young Nazis to climb into the trees and to make noises like birds. Huge sums of money had been extracted from the richer Jews and these sums had gone into the pockets of the Gauleiters. The mother of Prince Stahremberg had been forced to clean out the latrines at the Vienna railway station. Dr. Schuschnigg himself had been imprisoned. Vienna (that kindly capital) had in a night been turned into a place of brutality. "In any case," murmured the British, "it is not our affair."

The Czechs did not share this optimism. They knew that they were marked down as the next victim. Herr Hitler assured them that his intentions were strictly honourable. This sinister assurance made them shiver in their shoes.

CHAPTER VI

THE ROAD TO MUNICH

MARCH—SEPTEMBER, 1938

IT was the practice of George Joseph Smith, once he had selected a fresh bride, to begin operations by reassuring not only the lady herself, but her friends and relations. Herr Hitler adopts a similar technique. So long ago as March 7th, 1936, he had proclaimed that "Germany has no desire to attack either Poland or Czechoslovakia." A few weeks later he delivered an attack upon those critics of Nazi policy who had expressed doubt of his intentions. "The lie goes forth," he shouted, "that Germany to-morrow or the day after will fall upon Austria or Czechoslovakia. I ask myself always; who can these elements be who will have no peace, who incite continually, who must sow distrust, who want no understanding? Who are they?"

Who—indeed?

It was evident by March, 1938, to those who had some knowledge of the Führer's character and ambitions, that the rape of Austria would be but the prelude to a similar act of burglary with violence committed upon the, by then, encircled Czechoslovakia. Herr Hitler was quick to discredit such wicked suspicions. His assurances were both plausible and immediate; on March 14th, 1938, they were conveyed to the House of Commons by Mr. Chamberlain in the following words:

"I am informed that Field Marshal Goering on March 11th gave a general assurance to the Czech Minister in Berlin—an assurance which he expressly renewed on behalf of Herr Hitler—that it would be the earnest endeavour of the German Government to improve German-Czech relations. In particular on March 12th, Field Marshal Goering informed the Czech Minister that German troops marching into Austria had received the strictest orders to keep at least fifteen kilometres from the Czechoslovak frontier. On the same day the Czechoslovak Minister in Berlin was assured by Baron von Neurath that Germany considered herself bound by the German-Czechoslovak Arbitration Convention of October, 1925."

Even Mr. Chamberlain, who could scarcely be accused of "sowing distrust," does not appear, during those March days, to have been completely reassured. On March 24th, he admitted in the House of Commons that Europe had been faced by a "new situation" owing to the seizure of Austria, and to the "profound disturbances of international confidence" which that particular outrage had produced. While declining at that date to enter into any "automatic pledge" to any other prospective victims of Herr Hitler's rapacity, he made it clear "that if war broke out, it would be quite impossible to say where it would end." "This is," he added, "especially true in the case of two countries like France and Great Britain, with long associations of friendship, with interests closely interwoven, devoted to the same ideals of democratic liberty and determined to uphold them." The significance of this statement was as follows: (1) France was bound by treaty to Czechoslovakia, whereas, except under the League Covenant, Great Britain was not. (2) Great Britain was morally bound to France. (3) This statement on Mr. Chamberlain's part was, therefore, a warning to Herr Hitler that if he attacked Czechoslovakia, and if France came to her rescue, Great Britain would also become involved.

Why was it that such a warning, in March of 1938, appeared necessary? In order to answer that question I must explain as shortly as possible the general nature of the Czechoslovak problem.

Czechoslovakia lies (or lay) like some large lizard in the very middle of Europe. Her back rested against Poland; her tail dangled into Rumania; her stomach reposed uneasily upon Hungary and Austria; her nose protruded into Germany. It was her nose which was most important. In the first place, it was situated only 200 miles from Berlin. In the second place, it was something more than a nose; it was an extremely tough beak. This beak was stiffened, both on its upper and lower surfaces, by chains of mountains. Bismarck had described this frontier as "a fortress created by God himself," and the Czechs had improved upon the work of Providence by constructing along this frontier an impregnable Maginot line. It is not surprising that this frontier should have proved one of the most durable in history; it had subsisted for more than seven hundred years. Yet the beak of the Czechoslovak lizard, formidable though it was, possessed one great disadvantage. It was mottled by little islands of German settlers; their total number amounted to 3,500,000.

When, in 1918, the Czechs affirmed their independence and when the Peace Conference had, therefore, to determine the future frontiers of Czechoslovakia, the existence of these German colonies created a problem. It must be remembered that these "Sudeten Germans," as they were called, had never belonged to Germany; they had belonged to Austria. It was impossible to restore these islands to Austria, since great seas of purely Czech population intervened between. The Sudeten Germans did not, at the time, wish to join with Germany and even had they done so, such a cession would have been impossible not only for strategic, but also for economic, reasons. I was myself a member of the Committee of the Peace Conference which drew up the Czechoslovak frontiers. We were much bothered by this problem of the Sudeten Germans. What decided us was, first that this Bohemian frontier was a natural barrier which had existed for nearly a thousand years; and secondly (and more importantly), that the livelihood of these Germans depended upon their communications with the rest of Czechoslovakia. They could not, to put it simply, take their goods westward across the mountains into Germany; it was essential for them to continue, as before, to send their goods eastward to Prague. The old frontier was therefore preserved and the future status of these German populations was guaranteed under a Minorities Treaty by which Czechoslovakia undertook to respect their racial rights. It cannot be said that successive Czech governments carried out this engagement either in the spirit or in the letter.

2

In approaching this new victim Herr Hitler acted with caution. What he wanted to do, was to murder the victim and possess himself of her property. There were two considerations which he had to face. In the first place, the intended victim was herself sturdy, strong-minded and heavily protected; she might struggle in her bath. In the second place, she possessed powerful friends who might come to her assistance. A direct attempt at murder would certainly lead to trouble. He decided, therefore, to murder her by stages; and if possible to induce her friends to become accomplices in her assassination. He was successful in this stratagem.

The first thing to do was to undermine the victim's health and to convince her friends that she was about to die a natural death. The weak point in the victim's constitution was this pocket of Germans in her nose; Herr Hitler realised that if he sufficiently irritated this tumour it might become a malignant growth; cancer might follow. He laid his plans accordingly.

In 1935 he placed himself in contact with a young gymnastic instructor of the name of Konrad Henlein, who was a Sudeten German from the district of Asch in the Egerland. Henlein was instructed to reorganise the Sudeten Germans on Nazi lines and to tell all the Germans in Czechoslovakia how brutally they were being treated. He performed his task with energy and skill. The "German question" in Czechoslovakia, which in recent years had almost ceased to be a problem, suddenly became inflamed.

Herr Henlein, between 1935 and 1938, increased his influence and power. The seizure of Austria in March, 1938 (in that it exposed not only the sharp beak of Czechoslovakia but also its soft underside to attack) increased his confidence. On April 24th, 1938, in a speech at Karlsbad, he announced his terms. Six of the eight points which he then enunciated were quite reasonable; in them he claimed local self-government for the German minority in the Sudetenland. The other two were not reasonable. He demanded that the Sudeten Germans should be allowed to establish National Socialism, or in other words that they should, as Nazis, be allowed to suppress the Jews and their other political opponents. This would have created a state within the state. His eighth demand was equally unreasonable. He asked that the Czechoslovak Government should conform their foreign policy to the desires of Herr Konrad Henlein. In other words he demanded that the Prague Government should sever their connections with France, Russia and Great Britain and should place their country at the mercy of Germany. And this at the dictation of an alien minority.

A week after making this speech Herr Henlein came to England. He visited Mr. Winston Churchill and the opposition leaders. He paid me the honour of coming to my own chambers in the Temple. I invited a few fellow Members of Parliament (from every party) to meet him. We told him that although the mass of British opinion was in sympathy with his demand for local autonomy, we could not agree with the two last points in his Karlsbad programme. He assured us that these two points had been "mistranslated"; he had not the slightest intention of suppressing freedom of speech and action in the Sudetenland; he had no personal prejudice against the Jews or the Socialists. The autonomous area which he envisaged would be run on completely democratic lines. Nor had he ever intended to suggest that this small German minority would attempt to dictate the foreign policy of the whole Czechoslovak state. All he had meant by that point was that they would always oppose any anti-German policy on the part of Czechoslovakia. But, of course, they would oppose it only as a dissident minority, employing constitutional methods. We warned him that if he created a movement such as might lead Germany to violate Czechoslovak independence, Great Britain would go to war. We imagined, at the time, that in so warning him we were expressing the views of the Government and the country. He was assured in other British quarters that these warnings were merely the raving of the "warmongers." When, at the close of the discussion, I helped this stout schoolmaster into his enormous and ungainly greatcoat, I said to him: "I hope that you will not allow Hitler to render you the Seyss Inquart of Czechoslovakia." "Gott bewahre!" he answered, meaning by that "Good God, no!"

Such effect as these warnings (which were, of course, at once transmitted to Berlin) might or might not have produced upon Herr Hitler were discounted in the days that followed by two events. The Führer in the interval visited Rome; the Axis, which had been dislocated by the seizure of Austria, was reaffirmed. And at a luncheon-party in London Mr. Chamberlain assured the American journalists who were present that neither Great Britain, nor Russia nor even France would fight for the independence of

Czechoslovakia. An account of these assurances was published by Mr. Joseph Driscoll in the *Montreal Daily Star* of May 14th. It was at once relayed to Berlin. Herr Hitler thereupon prepared for action.

3

His first step was to launch against the Czechs a press campaign of the utmost virulence. They were described as the "bestial Czechs" and as the "truest friends of the Bolshevik murder rabble of the Kremlin." In every edition of the German newspapers reports were printed of the wholly imaginary tortures to which the Sudeten Germans were being exposed. At the same time, under the usual guise of manœuvres, German army corps were massed upon the frontier. On the night of May 20th–21st President Benes decreed partial mobilisation of the Czech army. The French Government issued a statement to the effect that "if Germany crosses the Czech frontier, that will automatically start war, and France will furnish help to the uttermost." Herr Hitler hesitated. Mutual appeasement was assayed. Herr Hitler sent his adjutant, Captain Wiedemann, to London. Mr. Chamberlain sent his friend, Lord Runciman, on an unofficial mission of mediation to Prague. The House of Commons adjourned in July under the impression that the May crisis had been successfully surmounted. "Throughout the continent," Mr. Chamberlain assured them, "there is a relaxation of that sense of tension which six months ago was present." There was, in fact, no relaxation. Throughout that July and August the German armies continued to take up positions which threatened Czechoslovakia from the south, west and north. The British Ambassador in Berlin was instructed on four separate occasions to make representations to the effect that "such abnormal measures could not fail to be interpreted abroad as a threatening gesture towards Czechoslovakia." The Czechoslovak Government, under pressure from Lord Runciman, then decided to meet Herr Henlein's demands, and produced what is known as "The Fourth Plan." This plan conceded practically all the points demanded by Herr Henlein in his Karlsbad speech. It was hoped at the time that this combination of conciliation and firmness might put an end to the dispute.

On September 7th, however, *The Times* newspaper (which is unjustly regarded abroad as the official organ of the Conservative Party) published a leading article suggesting that local self-government for the Sudeten Germans might not fully meet Herr Hitler's wishes, and that the Czech Government might be well advised to cede to Germany "that fringe of alien populations who are contiguous to the nations with which they are united by race." This article encouraged Hitler and Henlein to increase their demands; an incident was at once provoked at Moravska Ostrava; in his speech at Nürnberg on September 12th Herr Hitler launched a violent attack upon President Benes and the Czechoslovak Republic; and Herr Henlein broadcast an appeal for assistance against "the reign of terror of the Bolshevist Russite criminals in Prague," and declared the hour of liberation to be near. The crisis was drawing towards its climax.

On September 15th, 1938, Mr. Chamberlain flew to Berchtesgaden, hoping to persuade the Führer to

consent to a reasonable compromise. He was met
by an ultimatum. Herr Hitler by then had abandoned all pretence that what he desired was the
acceptance of the eight points of the Karlsbad
programme. He informed Mr. Chamberlain that
unless Czechoslovakia handed over to Germany the
whole frontier areas, including the Czech Maginot
line, Germany would seize these areas by force. On
Friday, September 16th, Mr. Chamberlain flew back
to London a sadder man. He at once summoned
the French ministers into conference. The result of
this duscussion was the drafting of the "Anglo-
French Plan." Under this plan the Czechs were to
surrender to Germany all sections of their country
which contained anything over 50 per cent Germans,
irrespective of whether these Germans wished or did
not wish to be incorporated under Nazi rule. The
Czechs replied that such a cession of their national
territory would be "tantamount to the mutilation of
their state," and they appealed to the German-
Czech Arbitration Treaty of 1925 which had recently
been reaffirmed by the Führer himself. Even *The
Times* newspaper, in its leader of September 20th,
admitted that the Anglo-French plan "could not, in
the nature of things, be expected to make a strong
prima facie appeal to the Czech Government, and
least of all to President Benes." It made no such
appeal. The Czechs refused to accept the plan. At
2.0 a.m. on Wednesday, September 21st, the French
and British ministers in Prague dragged Dr. Benes
from his bed. They informed him that unless the
Czechoslovak Government immediately accepted the
Franco-British plan he could expect no assistance
either from France or from Great Britain in the
war which would inevitably follow. The Czech

Government capitulated to this ultimatum addressed to them by their ally and their friend. In a broadcast to the Czech nation, President Benes informed his countrymen that he had been forced to yield "to pressure for which there is no precedent in history."

4

Having by these means obliged the Czechs to surrender their own defences, and thereby their own liberty, Mr. Chamberlain, accompanied by Sir Horace Wilson (industrial adviser to His Majesty's Government) flew to meet Herr Hitler at Bad Godesberg. It will be remembered that it was in this same hotel that the Führer in 1934 had plotted the murder of Röhm and his associates. On arrival at Bad Godesberg, Mr. Chamberlain was met by "a totally unexpected situation." He had imagined that Herr Hitler would feel deeply grateful to him for having forced the Czechs to surrender their defences and their frontiers. Herr Hitler now stated that the Anglo-French plan was out of date and presented further demands which were of so outrageous a nature that they came as "a profound shock" to Mr. Chamberlain. He consented none the less to transmit these demands to Prague. The Czech Government rejected these Godesberg demands as "absolutely and unconditionally inacceptable." The British Cabinet, on Mr. Chamberlain's return to London, also regarded the Godesberg ultimatum as something which no independent Government could accept and which the British Government could not ask them to accept. Mr. Chamberlain therefore despatched Sir Horace

Wilson to Berlin with a personal message to Herr
Hitler.

The Führer received Mr. Chamberlain's industrial
adviser in his Wilhelmstrasse office. Sir Horace
Wilson, in his gentle voice, began to read aloud the
message with which he had been entrusted. The
Führer slapped his thigh in rage, crossed his arms in
a gesture of incontrollable impatience, swung himself
sideways in his chair, gazed at the ceiling as if
appealing to Wotan and Thor and Odin to crush the
industrial adviser to His Majesty's Government, and
uttered the one word "*Schluss!*" That word is the
German equivalent of "Shut up." Again Sir Horace
Wilson tried to deliver his message. The Führer
raved and screamed. It was, he said, a matter of
days, nay of hours, nay of minutes. He refused to
delay for a moment longer. The conditions in the
Sudeten territories had become unbearable. His
personal honour and the honour of the whole
German nation was now involved. "I shall," he
screamed, "tear the Czechs into little pieces. They
must be smashed, smashed, smashed."

Sir Horace Wilson returned to London. The
Führer then announced that unless the Godesberg
terms were accepted by 2.0 p.m. on Thursday,
September 29th, that is in two days' time, Germany
would be obliged to take military action.

The intelligent reader will at this stage be asking
himself: "But what exactly was the difference between the Anglo-French plan and the terms embodied
in the Godesberg ultimatum? The difference was
as follows. The Anglo-French plan provided:

(*a*) That all areas containing a 51 per cent German
majority should be handed over to Germany.

(*b*) That the details of this transfer should be worked out by some international body, on which the Czechs should be represented.

(*c*) That France and Great Britain should guarantee the frontiers thereafter established. This meant that Czechoslovakia, having been forced to hand over her fortifications to Germany, would be protected from further assault by France and Great Britain.

The terms of the Godesberg ultimatum were:

(*a*) That the Czechs within a week should clear out of all the areas marked upon a map. These areas did not take any account of the 51 per cent German majority.

(*b*) That all German speaking soldiers in the Czech army should at once be discharged.

(*c*) That before November 25th a plebiscite should be held in other areas not marked on the map. The extent of these plebiscite areas was not defined.

(*d*) All Czech material, military or other as well as all live-stock and goods situated within the areas to be evacuated, must at once be handed over to Germany.

What did this mean? It meant that Czechoslovakia must at once surrender to Germany all those frontier districts in which her defences were situated. That, having thus been rendered defenceless, she would have to accept a "plebiscite" in a further unspecified area. And that all fortresses, guns, arms, war material, railways, rolling stock, etc., in the ceded area (including all farm produce) must be given to Germany at once. Obviously such terms could only be extracted from a beaten enemy.

On that evening of Tuesday, September 27th, Mr. Chamberlain delivered a broadcast address to the British nation. He referred to the plight of Czechoslovakia as "a quarrel in a far-away country between people of whom we know nothing." He contended rightly that the Anglo-French plan gave Germany "the substance of what she wanted." He cheered his audience (as also Herr Hitler) by assuring them that Great Britain was not prepared "in all circumstances" to go to war on account of Czechoslovakia. And he gave an assurance that "after this Sudeten German question is settled, that is the end of Germany's territorial ambitions in Europe."

CHAPTER VII

THE SEIZURE OF CZECHOSLOVAKIA

MARCH 15TH, 1939

THE French and British Governments, on that Tuesday, September 27th, 1938, were justifiably perturbed. The ultimatum issued that morning by Herr Hitler, as well as the unfriendly reception which he had given to Sir Horace Wilson, seemed to make it certain that German troops would march into Czechoslovakia on Thursday afternoon. The Czechs were determined to resist this invasion, and France would then be obliged either to come to their assistance, or else to violate a Treaty to which she was solemnly pledged. Great Britain, in that event, would be forced either to break her word of honour or to come to the help of France. A world war would result.

Hasty measures were taken to prepare for this danger. Children and old people were evacuated from Paris. In London and other British cities trenches were rapidly dug and gas masks were issued to the population. Parliament was summoned to meet in urgent session on the following afternoon. And just before midnight it was announced that the British fleet had been mobilised.

Appeals were also addressed to Herr Hitler from other quarters. President Roosevelt telegraphed a personal message to the Führer couched in serious and noble terms. Signor Mussolini, who had no wish whatsoever to engage his unwilling country in a war of Nazi ambition, was actively trying to persuade his partner in the Axis to desist from violent methods. Yet in all this diplomatic coming and going there was one ómission which remains to this day inexplicable. Russia, although herself bound both to Czecho-slovakia and France, was not invited to join the peace front. True it is that on September 23rd the British representatives to the League Assembly had some conversation with Litvinov. They asked him what Russia's attitude would be if France and Great Britain became involved in war with Germany on Czechoslovakia's behalf. M. Litvinov replied that in that event Russia would also come to the help of the Czechs and he even went so far as to suggest that military conversations should at once be opened between the French, British and Russian general staffs. This offer was transmitted to London but no reply was received. Throughout the ensuing negotiations the U.S.S.R. were ignored. This was a mistake.

At 2.45 p.m. on Wednesday, September 28th, the House of Commons assembled in a mood of anxiety and gloom. The Prime Minister, in carefully moderated phrases embarked upon a long account of the negotiations which had been carried on since the May crisis. He stood there at the table, resting the back of his left hand in the palm of his right, and reading quietly from the typescript spread upon the box before him. From time to time he would pick off his pince-nez between finger and thumb and gaze sadly upwards at the skylight. He seemed haggard and worn.

The House listened in silence to his long tale of

pledges broken and of warnings disregarded. The Prime Minister described his flight to Berchtesgaden and how, at his first meeting with Herr Hitler he had derived the impression that the Führer was prepared "to risk a world war" rather than to abate his demands. In desperation the French and British Governments had forced the Czechs to accept the "Anglo-French Plan" and to surrender their defences and their territory into German hands. Armed with this plan Mr. Chamberlain had flown to Godesberg. In spite of the fact that under this plan Herr Hitler obtained everything he had ever asked for, he still desired to attack the Czechs. He described the plan as "too dilatory," meaning thereby that under this scheme the Czechs would be given time to withdraw some, at least, of their livestock and munitions before the areas were occupied by German troops. "Imagine," the Prime Minister said, "the perplexity in which I found myself." This remark roused a murmur of sympathy on all benches. Mr. Chamberlain was touched by this demonstration. "It was," he added, "a profound shock to me." Again a murmur of sympathy passed along the crowded benches. He replaced his pince-nez, leaned forward towards the box on which his papers were spread out and continued his recital. The House waited in tense anxiety for him to reach the events of the last twelve hours. He reached them. "Yesterday morning," he began. . . .

At that moment a stir was noticed in the Peer's gallery. Lord Halifax, who had been listening intently, was suddenly seen to leave his place. A minute later a sheet of paper was passed down the Treasury bench. It was handed to Sir John Simon who glanced at it and then tugged at the Prime

Minister's coat.   Mr. Chamberlain ceased speaking,
adjusted his pince-nez, and read the document which
Sir John held up to him.   His whole features, his
whole body, seemed to change.   He raised his face
so that the light from the ceiling fell full upon it.   The
lines of anxiety and weariness seemed suddenly to
have been smoothed out.   For a few minutes longer
he continued his narrative of events.   And then he
disclosed the nature of the communication which he
had that moment received.   "I have," he said,
"something further to announce to the House yet.   I
have now been informed by Herr Hitler that he
invites me to meet him at Munich to-morrow morning.   He has also invited Signor Mussolini and M.
Daladier.   Signor Mussolini has accepted, and I
have no doubt M. Daladier will also accept.   I need
not say what my answer will be."

There was a momentary hush of astonishment
followed by an outburst of cheering such as the
House of Commons has seldom witnessed.   Members
of all parties rose in their places and waved the papers
in their hands.   It was then a quarter past four in the
afternoon.   The Prime Minister had been speaking
for over an hour.   After a few perfunctory words
from the leaders of the opposition, the House
adjourned.

A legend has since arisen that Mr. Chamberlain
was already aware when he began his speech that
Herr Hitler had agreed to postpone mobilisation and
to hold a Four Power Conference at Munich.
According to this legend the Prime Minister deliberately staged this dramatic surprise in order that the
House should be so completely swept off its feet as
to forget that our own safety was being purchased
at the price of Czechoslovakia's independence.

Nobody who actually saw the sudden transformation which passed across Mr. Chamberlain's tired features when he read that message, can believe this legend. Yet the fact remains that the House was so astonished and relieved that they adjourned without asking any further questions or demanding any guarantees. They did not realise in time that our honour and our safety were involved in maintaining the independence of this little Republic, of this strong natural bastion, against further German aggression. They were thinking (and who can blame them?) of those ghastly gas masks and those sodden little trenches in the parks. The Prime Minister left for Munich under the impression that the House of Commons desired only one thing; and that was peace at almost any price. I question whether it was a correct impression.

2

On Thursday, September 29th, 1938 (the day upon which the German ultimatum to Czechoslovakia had been due to expire) Mr. Chamberlain flew to Munich. He was joined by M. Daladier and Signor Mussolini. The Russian Government were not invited to attend these discussions. The Czech representatives who had also flown to Munich in order to be present at a conference which was to decide the fate of their country were not admitted to the conversations. The terms agreed to can be summarised as follows:

1. Czechoslovakia was to withdraw from her Maginot line and the adjoining territories in four stages, as between October 1st and October 7th.

2. An international Commission, composed of

Germany, Italy, France and Great Britain was to "lay down the conditions governing evacuation and to define forthwith the remaining territory of preponderatingly German character" in time for this also to be occupied not later than October 10th.

3.   The Czech Government was to be held responsible for any damage done to "existing installations." The exact meaning of that phrase was not defined.

4.   After these zones had been occupied by the German armies the Commission was to determine what other territory should be submitted to a plebiscite, at a date not later than the end of November, and to arrange for its occupation "by international bodies" until the completion of the voting.

5.   The Commission was also to carry out the final delimitation of the frontiers, but would be entitled to recommend to the four Powers "in certain exceptional cases minor modifications in the strictly ethnographical determination of the zones which are to be transferred without plebiscite."   In other words they might recommend that purely Czech areas should be annexed by Germany.

At 1.30 on the morning of Friday, September 30th, these terms were handed by Mr. Chamberlain and M. Daladier to the Czech representatives (M. Jan Masarik and M. Mastny), who until then had been confined in an anteroom.   Herr Hitler and Signor Mussolini were not present at this interview, feeling it more convenient, and infinitely more amusing, that the terms of surrender should be imposed upon the representatives of Czechoslovakia by that country's ally and friend.   The Czech representatives were not allowed to make any comment upon the sentence which had been passed upon them.   "It had," records M. Masarik, "been explained to us in a sufficiently brutal manner that it was a matter of condemnation without appeal and without possible modification."

Mr. Chamberlain, late on the following afternoon, alighted at Heston aerodrome. He emerged from the aeroplane waving a piece of paper above his head. "This," he exclaimed to the expectant microphone, "means peace in our time." He then drove to Buckingham Palace and came out upon the balcony to receive the ovations of the populace. His return to Downing Street was triumphal. He opened a window giving upon the street and addressed the crowds below him. "This is not," he said, "the first occasion on which a British Minister has returned from Germany bringing Peace with Honour." The crowds yelled their delighted approval. Some of Mr. Chamberlain's younger colleagues were so entranced by the occasion that they climbed up the lamp-post outside No. 10. There was one Cabinet Minister, at that time First Lord of the Admiralty, who took no share in this jubilation :

"On the last day," records Mr. Duff Cooper, "of September, 1938, the Prime Minister of Great Britain returned to London from Munich having concluded an agreement there which he hoped would form the basis of a lasting peace. It was a wet evening, but he was received as a conquering hero and his journey from the aerodrome to Whitehall was a triumphal progress. At Downing Street friends and colleagues were profuse in their congratulations. Even within the Cabinet no note of query or criticism was raised. . . . It was in these

circumstances and in the presence of my colleagues
that I felt it my duty to offer him my resignation.
It was not an easy or a pleasant task. . . . As I
walked back with one of my colleagues across the
Horse Guards Parade to Admiralty House, some
lingering remnant of that enthusiastic crowd recognised us and gave us a cheer, which I, at least, had
not merited."

On Monday, October 3rd, Mr. Duff Cooper in the
House of Commons explained the reasons for his
resignation. "The Prime Minister," he said, "has
confidence in the good-will and in the word of Herr
Hitler. . . . The Prime Minister may be right. I
can assure you, Mr. Speaker, with the deepest
sincerity, that I hope and pray that he is right. But
I cannot believe what he believes. I wish I could.
. . . I have given up the privilege of serving as Lieu-
tenant to a leader whom I still regard with the
deepest admiration and affection. I have ruined,
perhaps, my political career. But that is a little
matter; I have retained something which is to me of
great value—I can still walk about the world with my
head erect."

3

Some of the more virulent of Mr. Chamberlain's
critics have advanced the theory that when he spoke
of "Peace in our Time" and "Peace with Honour"
he was practising a deliberate deception upon both
the German and the British peoples. Their argument is that in that autumn of 1938, the state of our
defences was not such as to allow us to enter a major
war; that any frank discussion or disclosure of our

unpreparedness would not only encourage our enemies but do much damage to the Conservative party; and that therefore Mr. Chamberlain tried to "get away with it" by making a great virtue out of an unpleasant necessity. In other words, he was merely "playing for time."

I regard this criticism as ungenerous and untrue. Neither Mr. Chamberlain nor Sir Horace Wilson had experience of foreign politics, and their misconception of Herr Hitler's aims and character was absolutely sincere. I am convinced that the Prime Minister, on his return from Munich, really *did* believe that he had not only averted war but laid the foundations of peace. It may seem to some that a peace founded upon the betrayal and final coercion of a small country cannot accurately be described as "honourable." The point is whether the Prime Minister was justified at the time in regarding it as stable. According to the text of the agreements signed, and the assurances exchanged, he had some justification for this belief. Those of us who disagreed with his interpretation of the value of the Munich agreement were not basing our judgment upon the documents; we based it upon our knowledge of Herr Hitler's character. We felt certain that he would tear up the Munich agreement the moment that he found himself in the position to make a further attack.

The documents themselves, therefore, do not appear to me to be of primary importance, but they must be mentioned. I have already summarised the agreements regarding Czechoslovakia and it remains to indicate the nature of the piece of paper which Mr. Chamberlain had waved above his head when he arrived at Heston aerodrome. That document, which was signed by the Prime Minister and Herr Hitler, contained three clauses. Under the first clause they agreed "that the question of Anglo-German relations is of the first importance for the two countries and for Europe." Nobody would question the truth of this assertion. The second clause stated that "we regard the agreement signed last night and the Anglo-German Naval Convention as symbolic of the desire of our two peoples never to go to war with one another again." And the third clause ran as follows: "We are resolved that the method of consultation shall be the method adopted to deal with any other questions that may concern our two countries, and we are determined to continue our efforts to remove possible sources of differences and thus to contribute to assure the peace of Europe."

This somewhat illiterate document did not constitute a Treaty; it was little more than an expression of joint opinion coupled with assurances of mutual regard. Its value depended entirely upon the spirit in which it would be interpreted by Herr Hitler. In the very next speech which the Führer made, he rendered it abundantly clear that he himself did not attach any importance to this sheet of paper. Mr. Chamberlain, on the other hand, continued until March 15th, 1939, to regard it as the very charter of appeasement. To a critic who suggested that Herr Hitler had made many other promises in the past, he replied: "Yes, but on this occasion he has made them to *me*!"

It was customary at that time to make semi-humorous references to the conflict between the "appeasers" and the "war-mongers." There was no such conflict. There was no party, no group, no individual in Great Britain in favour of war. The only difference of opinion was between those who trusted Herr Hitler and those who did not trust Herr Hitler. If Hitler's word could be relied on, then perhaps the sacrifice of Czechoslovakia, shameful though it was, might not have been too heavy a price to pay for durable peace. But if Herr Hitler were merely following his usual practice of occupying strategical positions, and entering into treaties, for the sole purpose of gaining time and strength for some further act of spoilation, then France and Great Britain had sacrificed their honour, and one of the most formidable bastions in Europe, to no avail.

It is in the light of these considerations that the issue must be viewed. It would be beyond the purpose of this monograph to enter into any detailed arguments as to whether the terms imposed on the Czechs at Munich were, or were not, more favourable than the ultimatum addressed to them from Bad Godesberg. On paper they were certainly more favourable. Not only were the areas to be ceded to Germany, and the dates on which the Czechs had to retire from these areas, considerably modified, but the whole execution of the scheme was to be in the hands of an international commission consisting of representatives of the four powers. Moreover, the territory remaining to Czechoslovakia after this partition was to be guaranteed to them by Great Britain and France. This guarantee, in Mr. Chamberlain's words, would give Czechoslovakia, "a greater security than she had ever enjoyed in the past."

On paper, all this may well have been true. Herr Hitler does not pay much attention to paper promises. The International Commission, when it met in

Berlin, was composed of the Ambassadors of France, Great Britain and Italy plus the German Foreign Secretary. When this Commission came to define the areas, the Germans insisted upon enlarging their claims far beyond anything that had been contemplated at Godesberg. The Italian Ambassador was the only member of the Commission who had the courage to protest. It thus came about that the eventual territory seized by Germany was larger than anything that had been rejected at Godesberg. The Czechs, who had been tricked and bullied into surrendering all their fortresses, were incapable of any further defence. Their railway communications were severed, and 51 per cent of their coal mines were in German hands. The Germans also obtained 55 per cent of the·Czech glass industry, 49 per cent of their textile industry, one-third of the total industrial population of Czechoslovakia, and fourteen out of twenty-seven of their largest towns. Germany with the timid acquiesence of the French and British Ambassadors, acquired the whole of Czechoslovakia's Maginot line which had been erected at the cost of £50,000,000. And she succeeded in depriving the democracies of an ally, situated at a vital strategic point in the centre of Europe, and possessing a most efficient army of 1,500,000 men and 2,000 aeroplanes.

In the debate which followed in the House of Commons Mr. Winston Churchill summed up the results in a concise form. "The German Dictator," he said, "instead of snatching his victuals from the table has been content to have them served to him course by course. He demanded £1 from us at the pistol's point. When it was given, £2 was demanded at the pistol's point. Finally the Dictator consented to take £1 17s. 6d. and the rest in promises of good-will for the future. . . . We have suffered total and unmitigated defeat."

4

There remained the question of the guarantee of her future security which we had given to the trun-cated and dismembered state of Czechoslovakia. The Prime Minister, as has been said, described that guarantee as giving the Czechs greater security than they had enjoyed before. A few days later Sir Thomas Inskip announced on behalf of the Govern-ment that they felt "under a moral obligation to treat that guarantee as being now in force." The British Cabinet may have been encouraged to assume and to reaffirm this moral obligation by the words of a speech delivered two days before by Herr Hitler. "I shall not," he said, "be interested in the Czecho-slovak State any more." Peace, it would seem, had been secured.

The relief with which the British people had hailed the Munich settlement was not of long duration. Throughout the crisis they had tried to persuade themselves that all that Herr Hitler wanted was to free the Sudeten Germans from Czech rule. When the maps were published showing the exact territory which the Ambassadors had given to Germany it was found that the ethnographical limit had in every case been exceeded and that under the guise of "self-determination," Germany had possessed herself of the whole defences, most of the industrial areas, and most of the vital railway junctions in Bohemia and Moravia. Further spoliation of Czech territory was carried out by the Hungarians and the Poles.

President Benes, whose conduct throughout had earned him the admiration of the world, was forced to resign and leave the country. The American Press was unanimous in expressing horror at the perfidy of France and the weakness of England. It gradually came to be realised in Great Britain that we had suffered a deep and dangerous humiliation. Our pride was wounded. We could not accept such humiliation again.

Nor were our anxieties in regard to Hitler's own intentions for long allayed. Speaking at Saarbrücken on October 9th the Führer delivered a violent attack on Mr. Churchill, Mr. Eden and Mr. Duff Cooper and asserted that "it would be well if people in England gave up certain airs and graces of the Versailles epoch. We will not tolerate admonitions to Germany as by a governess. Statesmen should concern themselves with their own affairs and should not continually take a hand in the problems of other countries." This speech was scarcely in the best Munich spirit as that spirit was interpreted in London. Moreover, it was perplexing to many people to observe that the Prime Minister, having achieved "peace in our time," suddenly embarked upon an armament programme such as we had never before undertaken in time of peace.

Stories began gradually to filter through regarding the atrocities being perpetrated by the Henleinists upon the Jews and socialists. As early as September 30th Herr Henlein had announced that "Such men have no right to justice. We shall imprison them until they turn black." A vast concentration camp was created at Bodenbach. The reign of Nazi terror had begun in the provinces which had been acquired.

Herr Hitler, meanwhile (grateful though he was

for the vast strategic and economic advantages which he had been given), was desperately short of cash. The murder of von Rath by a young Jew in Paris gave him his opportunity. At 2.0 a.m. on November 10th he launched a pogrom against the whole Jewish community in Germany and Austria. Thousands of Jews were herded into concentration camps, where they were exposed to obscene treatment. And as a fine for the murder for which they were in no sense responsible the Jewish community were mulcted of the fantastic sum of £83,000,000. Yet even this enormous levy did not give Herr Hitler all the cash that he required.

A large proportion of the sums paid never found their way into the state coffers, but were intercepted by Nazi officials for their private use. More loot was needed. And thus in these winter months Herr Hitler silently, slowly, shrewdly, planned the murder of Prague.

The British Government, in spite of the fact that the Jewish persecution had convinced most Europeans of the criminality of the Nazi system, remained confident that the spirit of Munich still persisted. In the first week of March a Press conference was held at 10, Downing Street, and the assembled journalists were assured that never had appeasement shown greater successes and that an era of peace was at last about to descend upon Europe. Encouraged by these assurances, the Editor of *Punch* instructed Mr. Bernard Partridge to design a happy cartoon for their issue of Wednesday, March 15th. This cartoon, which was entitled "The Ides of March," depicted John Bull waking up from an appalling nightmare. The nightmare was itself shown escaping through the window in the guise of a scare-monger. John Bull exclaimed: "Thank God! That's over!"

It was not over. On the very day that this cartoon appeared the German troops burst into Prague. The final murder of Czechoslovakia was accomplished.

5

Herr Hitler, in carrying out this assassination, adhered strictly to his accustomed technique. He began by assurances. "In general," he said a Berchtesgaden on January 1st, 1939, "we have but one wish—that in the coming year we may be able to make our contribution to the general pacification of the whole world." Yet on March 10th a rising against the Prague Government was organised in Slovakia. Disorders were also created at Iglau and Brno. On March 13th the German armies in Bavaria and Austria moved up to the Czech frontier. And on March 14th the President of the Czecho-slovak Republic, M. Hacha, received orders to come to Berlin immediately. He arrived at 10.0 p.m. and was taken to Herr Hitler's office. Throughout the night he was subjected to third-degree methods in the hope of forcing him to sign away what remained of Czech independence. Twice did he faint under the ordeal to which he was being subjected, but Herr Hitler had thoughtfully seen to it that a doctor should be in attendance in the next room. At 3.0 a.m. the President was informed that unless he signed immediately orders would at once be given for 800 aeroplanes, which were being held in readiness, to destroy the city of Prague. At 3.55 a.m. President Hacha collapsed. He signed the following document:

"The Czechoslovak President has declared that in order to reach a final pacification, he would place the fate of the Czech people and their country confidently in the hands of the Führer of the German Reich."

He had, of course, no constitutional right to do anything of the sort.

At 6.0 a.m. on March 15th the German armies occupied Bohemia and Moravia. Hitler himself entered Prague at 7.15 that evening. The Czechoslovak Republic was extinguished. And in London Mr. Chamberlain explained that our moral guarantee could hardly be expected to apply to something which had ceased to exist.

The loot which Herr Hitler obtained from this second murder was considerable. He acquired a potential increase in man-power of 15,000,000; great agricultural resources; enormous reserves of timber; the whole industry of Bohemia and Moravia; the Skoda armament works, large stocks of guns and munitions, many aeroplanes; and, above all, gold and foreign credits to the total of £60,000,000. His had been a most profitable victory, and he had won it without sacrificing the bones of a single grenadier.

6

The Ides of March came as a profound shock to British opinion. Hitherto the great mass of ordinary, decent-minded folk had believed in the policy of appeasement. They cherished nothing but feelings of good-will towards the German people and they asked only to live on terms of peace and amity with Germany for the rest of time. Hitherto, on every occasion when Herr Hitler had broken a treaty, they had given him the benefit of the doubt. His denunciation of Locarno and his military occupation of the Rhineland, had, it is true, been something of a shock—but had not Germany the moral right to fortify her own territory? The occupation of Vienna may have been carried out in rather a high-handed manner, but had not the Austrians always been anxious to join the Reich? The pressure put upon the wretched Czechs at the time of the Munich crisis had undoubtedly been harsh and humiliating, but then how could you expect a great country such as Germany to allow her brothers across the frontier to remain under a foreign yoke? Always, until March 15th, there had been some argument, some excuse, which enabled the ordinary peaceful person to pretend to himself that there was nothing abnormal about Herr Hitler's methods or ambitions, and that, if only we were patient, he would quiet down in time. The seizure of Prague changed all that. In twelve hours the great majority of people in England realised that the policy of appeasement had failed completely. We had permitted the dictator Powers to gain control over China, Abyssinia, Spain, the Rhineland, Austria and Czechoslovakia in the hopes that by our complacency we might gain their friendship. All we had gained was the contempt of friend and foe alike. It was now clear that Herr Hitler was out for loot and conquest. The dreadful day might come when he would cease murdering small and distant countries of which we knew little, and start attacking us. The British public became both angry and alarmed.

For Mr. Chamberlain, Herr Hitler's destruction of the Munich agreement was something more than a national, or even a universal, disaster: it was a personal affront. From the very day when he had succeeded Mr. Baldwin at No. 10, Downing Street, Mr. Chamberlain had taken into his own hands the steering wheel of foreign policy. Instead of the middle course which had been followed by previous statesmen, he struck off on a new line, veering well to starboard, and avoiding the cranks, the experts and the sentimentalists on the port side. He was, he explained, a "realist" in foreign affairs. This constant opposition to the Dictators could only end in trouble; the line to take was to talk to the Dictators as man to man, to try and understand their point of view, to try to satisfy their reasonable aspirations; and meanwhile not to annoy or irritate them by any outspokenness, by any press or parliamentary indiscretions, by any too overt sympathy with provocative things such as collective security, the League of Nations, the independence of small countries, the Spanish republicans, or the U.S.S.R. As the months passed Mr. Chamberlain became more and more personally identified with his own policy. Mr. Anthony Eden ventured to doubt whether Signor Mussolini was keeping the agreement not to intervene in the Spanish civil war; he was obliged to resign his post as Foreign Secretary. Mr. Duff Cooper ventured to doubt whether Herr Hitler would keep to the pledges which he had given at Munich; he also retired from the Cabinet. Mr. Chamberlain merely gripped the steering wheel more firmly and continued upon the course that he had chosen. He might well have succeeded. Had he been dealing with men of even average reason or good faith it might have been that under his firm guidance the ship of state would have reached the blessed isles of peace. There are many wise people who even to-day feel that the experiment was worth making and that Mr. Chamberlain's unswerving integrity of purpose has given his country a clear conscience with which to face the ordeals which are to come. That may be so. No sane person can doubt the purity of the Prime Minister's intentions. The only thing that was lacking was an understanding of the true nature of the Nazi movement. Mr. Chamberlain imagined that he was dealing with a national revival; he was really dealing with a world revolution, led by an almost demented fanatic. He and his adviser, Sir Horace Wilson, stepped into diplomacy with the bright faithfulness of two curates entering a pub for the first time; they did not observe the difference between a social gathering and a rough house; nor did they realise that the tough guys therein assembled did not either speak or understand their language. They imagined that they were as decent and as honourable as themselves.

The first days of March had found the Prime Minister still steering confidently upon the course of appeasement. The sky was clear, the winds seemed favourable, the glass was going up. Then suddenly, on March 15th, there was a sound of breakers ahead. With commendable promptitude Mr. Chamberlain reversed his course. Two days after the seizure of Prague he spoke at Birmingham and voiced, not only his own feelings, but the doubts and apprehensions of the whole people. "Is this," he said, "the end of an old adventure or the beginning of a new? Is this the last attack upon a small state or is it to be followed by others? Is this in fact a step in the direction of an attempt to dominate the whole world by force?"

It was not the last attack. Even as Mr. Chamberlain was speaking Herr Hitler was planning the murder of Poland.

CHAPTER VIII

THE SEIZURE OF POLAND

SEPTEMBER 1ST, 1939

POLAND, throughout her long life, has suffered much from the fact that she possesses no natural frontiers and is therefore liable to excite the cupidity of her eastern and her western neighbours. Three times during the eighteenth century did Germany and Russia conspire together to despoil Poland for their own advantage. In 1772 they took a little; in 1793 they took some more; in 1796 they took the whole. Poland by this last partition was wiped off the map, and (except for a brief interlude under Napoleon) she lost her independence for one hundred and twenty-two years. She did not, however, lose her identity. From 1796 until 1918 the Poles waited with resolute confidence for the moment when their nation should be restored to them. That moment came on November 3rd, 1918, when the new Republic of Poland was proclaimed with Paderewski as its first President.

The Peace Conference in Paris had a difficult task in fixing the frontiers of this resurrected Poland. No. 13 of President Wilson's Fourteen Points had laid it down that an independent Polish state should be created "which should include territories inhabited by indisputably Polish populations, and which should be assured a free and secure access to the sea." The German Government accepted this principle as one of the conditions of peace. It is inaccurate of Herr Hitler to pretend that the whole Polish settlement was imposed upon a beaten Germany by the Versailles dictators. Germany of her own free will agreed, before she laid down her arms, that the future Poland should include all Polish populations and should be accorded "free and secure" access to the sea.

The problem of how to achieve this end was one of great difficulty. The only sea to which Poland could possibly be given access was the Baltic. The only means by which she could obtain this access was along her great river the Vistula. Yet at the very mouth of the Vistula was situated the German city of Danzig. How, therefore, was such access to be not only "free" but also "secure"? It was as if England's only outlet to the sea was along the Thames and as if Tilbury and Gravesend were inhabited by German majorities. The first idea was to break through this difficulty and to cede Danzig to Poland in spite of its predominantly German population. Mr. Lloyd George was opposed to this solution. Another plan was tried. It was known that the territory to the west of the Vistula was inhabited by an indisputably Polish population. It was decided, therefore, that this territory should become part of the Polish state. It was also decided that Danzig should be created a free and unarmed city under a High Commissioner appointed by the League of Nations with a Senate and constitution of her own. By this means Poland obtained a corridor to the sea inhabited by predominately Polish populations. She also obtained the use, under certain conditions, of the harbour of Danzig. It was felt that by these means President Wilson's thirteenth point had been fulfilled; Poland had not been allowed to annex a German city; yet she obtained by the device of the corridor and the self-governing city of Danzig what ought certainly to have been "free and secure" access to the sea.

This settlement has been criticised on the ground that the Polish corridor sunders the German province of East Prussia from direct land communication with the Reich. New Zealand is even more sundered from the mother country, and many miles of British Columbia intervene between Alaska and the United States. Yet from 1919 to 1933 "Danzig and the Corridor" became one of the commonplaces of German propaganda against the Treaty of Versailles. It was expected that the first thing which Adolf Hitler would do when he came to power was to denounce this arrangement. He did the exact opposite. His first major diplomatic operation was to reaffirm it.

On January 26th, 1934, he signed an agreement with Poland under which the arrangement regarding Danzig and the corridor was to remain unchanged for a period of ten years. He undertook during that period not to seek to alter the existing settlement by force. In the years that followed he constantly reaffirmed that obligation. On February 20th, 1938, he boasted in the Reichstag that the 1934 agreement "had taken the poison out of the relations between Germany and Poland" and that "this dangerous spot from the point of view of European peace has entirely lost its menacing character." In the following September he announced that his Treaty with Poland had "entirely removed the danger of conflict." And as recently as January,

1939, he had assured the Reichstag that "during the troubled months of the past year the friendship between Germany and Poland was one of the reassuring factors in the political life of Europe."

In spite of these assurances the British Government were certain that after the rape of Czechoslovakia, Poland would be the next victim. Until then they had tried hard to believe that Hitler was seeking only to secure his rights; after the seizure of Prague they realised that his aim was to seize the rights of others. Even as Czechoslovakia had left her frontiers against Austria almost undefended, so also had Poland considered it unnecessary to create strong defensive positions against Czechoslovakia. Hitler had kicked the Czechs in the stomach; the stomach of Poland was now exposed. Her strategic position was immeasurably weakened by the disappearance of Czechoslovakia as an independent Power. It was feared, both in London and at Warsaw, that Herr Hitler might strike a sudden blow while the armies which he had mobilised for the seizure of Prague were still in being.

2

The tactics adopted by the Führer were subtle and dilatory. His first manœuvre was an attempt to put Poland in the wrong. On March 21st (the very day that Memel was occupied) Herr von Ribbentrop in conversation with the Polish Ambassador in Berlin suggested that immediate discussions might be opened between Germany and Poland for the purpose of finding a permanent solution of the Danzig problem. He stated that Danzig must be given to Germany who must also obtain a band of territory across the corridor. In return for this Germany would promise to respect Polish economic interests and would accord her a non-aggression pact lasting for twenty-five years. The Polish Government were alarmed by this conversation, and on March 23rd they took defensive measures upon their frontier. Three days later they replied to the German suggestion by offering counter-proposals under which Poland and Germany should jointly guarantee the special status of Danzig and under which Germany would obtain all possible transit facilities across the corridor short of actual transference of territory. Herr Hitler subsequently informed the Reichstag that he had interpreted these counter-proposals as "displaying an entire lack of comprehension for the German point of view and as equivalent to a rejection of the German proposals." He therefore returned no reply to Poland for a month. Let me restate this first episode in simpler terms: (1) Hitler was pledged by his treaty with Poland not to raise the question of Danzig or the corridor until 1944. (2) After seizing Czechoslovakia, he calmly informed Poland that they must at once give him Danzig and allow him to cut the corridor in half. (3) When, instead of accepting these demands outright, the Poles put forward counter-proposals, he lay low for a month and then accused them of having refused to discuss the matter.

That was the first move. The second move came from London.

On March 31st the Prime Minister made an important statement in the House of Commons. He referred to the rumours of a projected attack upon Poland and repeated his hope that the Danzig difficulty might be settled by direct negotiation between Warsaw and Berlin. He added these words: "In the event of any action which clearly threatened Polish independence, and which the Polish Government accordingly considered it vital to resist with their national forces, His Majesty's Government would feel themselves bound at once to lend the Polish Government all support in their power. They have given the Polish Government an assurance to that effect."

This was a vital pronouncement. It meant that he had given a public pledge to Poland that we should go to war with Germany if the latter took such action as would clearly threaten Polish independence. It was, perhaps, unfortunate that before giving this guarantee the Prime Minister had not thought fit to approach the Russian Government and to make quite certain that they would join us in this tremendous and unusual obligation. The Russian Ambassador in London was, it is said, only informed of Mr. Chamberlain's declaration three hours before it was made.

Herr Hitler, as was to be expected, was enraged by our intervention. At Wilhelmshaven, on April 1st, he delivered a fulminating speech against Great Britain. "Germany," he said, "does not dream of attacking other nations. We have given great happiness to Central Europe, namely peace, peace protected by German power. And this power shall not be broken by any force in the world. That is our oath. . . . He who does not possess power loses the right to live." "The German people," he added, "was created by Providence not in order to obey a law which suits Englishmen and Frenchmen, but to stand for its vital right. That is what we are

there for! . . . If they expect Germany of the
present day patiently to allow vassal states, whose
only duty consists in being set to work against
Germany to carry on as they like, then they are
confounding present-day Germany with the Germany
of pre-war days."

In spite of this fulmination, Herr Hitler remained
comparatively quiescent for four weeks. On April
28th he made his second move. The first thing he
did was to denounce the Anglo-German Naval
Agreement of 1935 on the ground that we were
seeking to "encircle" him. The second thing he
did was to address a furious Note to Poland. The
British Government's declaration of their intention
to conclude with Poland a Pact of mutual assistance
showed that "Poland prefers a promise of help by a
third Power to the direct guarantee of peace by the
German Government." She did indeed. Herr
Hitler accordingly denounced the German Polish
Treaty which he had himself negotiated and signed
in 1934. The Polish Foreign Secretary, Colonel
Beck, replied to this onslaught on May 5th. He
pointed out that there was nothing in the 1934
treaty which forbade Poland to make friends with
other countries. He added that Poland was always
willing to negotiate a new treaty with Germany
provided that she was assured of Germany's "peaceful intentions and peaceful methods of procedure."
In a Note which he addressed to the German Government on the same day he repeated these assurances
but maintained his refusal to be bullied into one-
sided concessions. "It is clear," he wrote, "that
negotiations in which one State formulates demands
and the other is obliged to accept these demands un-
altered are not negotiations in the spirit of the

declaration of 1934 and are incompatible with the vital interests and dignity of Poland."

In the meanwhile certain other moves had been made elsewhere. On April 7th, Signor Mussolini, who did not see why Hitler should have all the fun to himself, seized Albania by force. On April 13th, Great Britain extended her guarantee to Rumania and Greece, and a few days later opened negotiations with both Russia and Turkey. The negotiations with Turkey were brilliantly successful and an agreement was drafted by May 12th. The Russian negotiations were not so fortunate. They had scarcely been opened when M. Litvinov, who was known to be in favour of a peace front against Germany, was suddenly dismissed from office. The British Government appear to have taken this event with calm. Instead of pressing on the negotiations for an Anglo-Russian pact they waited six weeks before sending a special emissary to Moscow. And even then it was not Lord Halifax, or some other Minister of Cabinet rank, who was despatched, but a gifted though subordinate official of the Foreign Office.

3

Looking back on events in the light of the published documents, one now sees that the Polish crisis was actually divided into two stages with a three months lull in between. The first stage lasted from March 21st to April 28th. The second stage did not really begin till August 3rd. During this three months interval the centre of gravity shifted from Danzig, Warsaw, Paris and London to the Kremlin. The struggle became a struggle for the

Russian alliance. The British Government did not fully realise the intensity of this struggle at the time. It seems probable that the Führer, flushed by his seizure of Prague and Memel, hoped at one moment to win a fourth white war and to force Poland to surrender before her friends could come to her assistance. He was checked in this attempt, partly by the firm resistance of the Polish Government, partly by Mr. Chamberlain's outspoken assurance, and partly by the dread of an Anglo-Russian agreement.

It must always be borne in mind that Adolf Hitler resembles George Joseph Smith in this also, that he does not really enjoy shooting his brides; what he enjoys is to poison them a little and then to strangle them with his white and flabby hands. He had managed to strangle Austria, Czechoslovakia and Memel without shedding a drop of blood. Poland was not so easy. In the first place she would struggle and shout for help. In the second place her friends and relations were, by now, acutely suspicious and would rush to her rescue. The only thing to do was to persuade the closest and largest of her relations to become an accomplice to the murder; this would frighten more distant relations away. Herr Hitler therefore instructed his Ambassador in Moscow, Count Schulenburg to make secret overtures to Stalin. The dismissal of Litvinov on May 3rd may well have been the first blossom of a conspiracy which was to bear such bitter fruits.

The Führer, as he informed Sir Neville Henderson a few weeks later, is a man of "*ad infinitum* decisions." His knowledge of Latin is faulty, but he meant by this that he was a man who would stop at nothing. An agreement between Hitler and Stalin, between the

Nazis and the Bolsheviks, was indeed a proposition which might have made the most cynical, the most reckless spirit quail. It entailed terrific dangers.

It entailed, in the first place, the repudiation of his whole doctrine. For six years he had imposed great sufferings on his people by persuading them that it was Germany who must lead the crusade against the "scum of humanity," the "myrmidons of hell," the "liars and lunatics" "the bloodstained criminals" of Moscow. For this great cause Horst Wessel and countless other boys had died; for this great cause thousands had been executed, or crushed to spiritual death in concentration camps; for this great cause young Germans had given their lives in Spain. Would even the German people retain their confidence in a leader who, for purposes which they could not understand or share, suddenly changed the whole message which for six long years he had dinned into their souls? Had he not himself, in *Mein Kampf*, proclaimed that an agreement between Russia and Germany would mean the end of his own country? Could even *his* legend survive such frightful inconsistency?

It entailed in the second place the renunciation of his immediate ambitions. Russia would demand a heavy price. She would demand a large slice of Poland. She would demand supreme influence over the Baltic States. And above all she would demand the abandonment of Hitler's dream of a "Drive to the east" and would cut him off, perhaps for ever, from the mouths of the Danube and the Black Sea.

It entailed in the third place the betrayal of his friends. Japan would be outraged by this change of course and might be driven back into the arms of

England. Spain, in which good German blood had been shed, would be alienated by such treachery. And Italy, a deeply Catholic country, would feel herself abandoned and betrayed.

In the fourth place it would expose him to serious internal dangers. The virus of bolshevism would be spread throughout Germany and the vitality of his country would, if a long war followed, be slowly sapped. He must have foreseen that Stalin's sole object was to secure that Germany and England should wear each other out. Russia could never in any circumstances allow Germany to triumph in a second world war. Nor, if communism threatened, would the German Army retain indefinitely their loyalty to this little Bohemian corporal. The moment might come when they would join with France and England in stamping out the fires which he had so cynically lit.

It is not possible, as yet, to be certain of the motives which impelled the Führer to this amazing reversal of his doctrine. Is it that he was merely playing a clever diplomatic trick and desired to outwit British statesmen by outbidding them at Moscow? Is it that he has always been a communist at heart and that the deception which all his life he has practised upon the German people was a deliberate and long-meditated deception? Is it that he seriously believed that France and Great Britain would be so frightened by the Russian bogey that they would, without striking a blow, abandon Poland to his hands? Or is it that he is, in fact, a second Jenghiz Khan intent upon conquest to any limit and at any price, and dreaming of securing for himself the whole might and riches of the French and British Empires?

The motives which inspired Stalin are far easier to understand. At only two points is the U.S.S.R. sensitive to attack, namely in the Black Sea and the Baltic. The increasing power of Nazi Germany filled Russia with alarm. There was a time when she would gladly have joined with the Western Powers in combating this common danger. Her overtures were rejected and her envoys snubbed. When England and France allowed Czechoslovakia to fall without a blow, when it became clear that the fortifications of the Rhineland had rendered Germany almost impervious to any land attack from the west, the Russians began to wonder whether it would not be more prudent to make terms with the enemy at their gates than to rely upon the assistance of such timid, distant and withal patronising friends. The Germans and the Russians have always possessed a strange affinity; Russia is one of the few countries which really understands Germany, and perhaps the only country which Germany knows how to handle; and the differences which (however Hitler might scream and rave) existed between the Nazi and the Bolshevik systems were, in fact, no greater that those which separate Woolworths from Marks and Spencer. One of them is painted red.

On August 21st the world was startled to learn that Germany had signed a pact with Russia. On September 1st the German armies invaded Poland.

4

The final stages in this drama need not be recorded in any great detail. By the end of July Herr Hitler appears to have been confident that he would get his

Russian alliance and to have staged the murder of Poland in the usual way. On July 25th notices were issued calling up the German reservists for the second fortnight in August and steps were taken by the local Nazis (who had obtained complete control over the city) to place Danzig in a state of defence. The usual measures were adopted to inflame local feeling, and if possible to irritate the Polish authorities into taking steps which could be interpreted as "provocation." On August 4th, the Polish customs inspectors were informed by the Senate of Danzig that henceforward they would not be allowed to carry out their duties. The Polish Government replied by a firm protest pointing out that such action was a violation of the Statute of Danzig. The Senate, much to everybody's surprise, gave way to this protest. Four days later, the German Government intervened in this dispute. They described the Polish protest as "in the nature of an ultimatum" and such "as will lead to an aggravation of German Polish relations, for the consequence of which the responsibility will fall exclusively upon the Polish Government." A terrific press campaign was then launched in the German Press and the Poles were accused of exposing German nationals to persecution and torture such as the Führer could no longer tolerate. The world, by then, was familiar with these opening moves. They knew all too well what they portended.

The British Government did all within their power to prevent a collision. While urging restraint at Warsaw, they addressed repeated warnings to Berlin. So long ago as May 28th our Ambassador in Berlin had told Field Marshal Göring that "as a result of the Prague coup, His Majesty's Government and the

British people were determined to resist any further aggression. If Germany endeavoured to settle the question of Danzig and the corridor by unilateral action such as would compel the Poles to resort to arms to safeguard their independence, we and the French as well as other countries would be involved with all the disastrous consequences which a world war would entail." Similar warnings were uttered by Lord Halifax on June 29th, by the Prime Minister on July 10th, and by our Ambassador on July 14th. Herr Hitler may well have believed that such warnings would become meaningless once he had secured his pact with the U.S.S.R. He was quickly disillusioned. On August 22nd, on the very day after the conclusion of the Russo-German pact, Mr. Chamberlain wrote a personal letter to Herr Hitler in which he warned him that "whatever be the nature of the German-Soviet agreement, it cannot alter Great Britain's obligation to Poland."

"Having thus," he continued, "made our position perfectly clear, I wish to repeat to you my conviction that war between our two peoples would be the greatest calamity that could occur. I am certain that it is desired neither by our people, nor by yours, and I cannot see that there is anything in the questions arising between Germany and Poland which could not and should not be resolved without the use of force, if only a situation of confidence could be restored to enable discussions to be carried on in an atmosphere different from that which prevails to-day. "We have been, and at all times will be, ready to assist in creating conditions in which such negotiations could take place, and in which it might be possible concurrently to discuss the wider problems affecting the future of international relations, including matters of interest to us and to you."

With this in mind Mr. Chamberlain appealed for "a truce on both sides—and indeed on all sides—to press polemics and to all incitement."

This letter was taken by Sir Neville Henderson to Berchtesgaden. He saw Herr Hitler on August 23rd and found him "excitable and uncompromising." "He was not," he said, "interested in our offer of a general negotiation on points interesting our two countries." On the other hand the persecutions of his fellow Germans in Poland must cease immediately and the questions of Danzig and the corridor "must and shall be solved." On the following day our Ambassador had another interview with the Führer and found him in a calmer but no less determined mood. Hitler made two astounding assertions. The first was that "he was now fifty years old and preferred war now to when he was fifty-five or sixty." The second was that "England was fighting for far lesser races whereas he was fighting only for Germany." These two remarks indicate how tragically Herr Hitler misconceived our point of view.

Meanwhile, the leaders of world opinion endeavoured by general appeals to the interested Powers to prevent the calamity which appeared to be approaching. On August 23rd the King of the Belgians broadcast an appeal for peace on the part of the Oslo Group of Powers. His Holiness the Pope issued a similar appeal from the Vatican on August 24th. President Roosevelt went further. On August 23rd he telegraphed a suggestion to the King of Italy begging him to formulate proposals for a pacific solution. The King's reply, seven days later, was curt and non-committal. On August 24th President Roosevelt addressed a more detailed message to Herr Hitler and to the President of Poland. He begged them to "refrain from any positive act of hostility for a reasonable stipulated period" and meanwhile to make an attempt to solve their common difficulties either by direct negotiation, by arbitration, or by conciliation. He offered the assistance of the United States towards that end.

"I appeal to you," he wrote, "in the name of the people of the United States, and I believe in the name of peace-loving men and women everywhere, to agree to a solution of the controversies existing between your Government and that of Poland through the adoption of one of the alternative methods I have proposed."

President Moscicki replied at once accepting President Roosevelt's proposals. The President then telegraphed this acceptance to Herr Hitler and begged him also to agree. "All the world," he wrote, "prays that Germany too will accept."

Herr Hitler did not accept.

He must have been convinced by then that, in spite of the Russo-German pact, Great Britain was determined to honour her obligation to Poland. He attempted, in a clumsy fashion, to buy us off. In a long and excited letter which he sent to our Ambassador he assured him that Germany could no longer tolerate the "Macedonian conditions" on her Eastern border, and was determined to settle Poland once and for all. So soon, however, as this had been accomplished, he was ready to approach Great Britain with "a large comprehensive offer." "He is," he said (referring modestly to himself in the third person) "a man of great decisions and in this case also will be capable of being great in his actions. He accepts the British Empire and is ready to pledge himself to its continued existence."

The British Government may well have felt that the continued existence of the British Empire was dependent upon factors more durable and potent than the good-will of Adolf Hitler. Their reply was courteous but firm. They were prepared, they said, to accept a general discussion provided that the differences between Germany and Poland were first peacefully composed. "They could not," their note added, "for any advantage offered to Great Britain, acquiesce in a settlement which put in jeopardy the independence of a State to whom they have given their guarantee." In handing this reply to Herr Hitler our Ambassador added that "our word was our word and we had never, and would never break it." He reminded him that a great German, Marshal Blücher, had in almost that exact phrase described the German conception of national honour. "That may be," replied Adolf Hitler, "but things were different one hundred and twenty-five years ago."

At 7.15 p.m. on August 29th the Führer handed to Sir Neville Henderson Germany's final reply. The interview, our Ambassador records "was of a stormy character." It is clear that Herr Hitler had by then decided to attack Poland immediately and regardless of the consequences. His final actions were no more than attempts to manœuvre Poland and Great Britain into the wrong. He agreed to open direct negotiations with Poland but insisted that a Polish emissary "with full powers" must reach

Berlin on the following day. The Polish Government were unwilling to expose Colonel Beck to the humiliations and sufferings which had been imposed upon Schuschnigg and Hacha. They knew all about third degree methods. They asked that direct negotiations might take place through the ordinary diplomatic channels. We supported them in that request. At midnight, on August 30th, the German Foreign Minister read out to Sir Neville Henderson the terms which *would have* been given to the Polish plenipotentiary had he arrived. These terms were not in themselves excessive; the point about them is that they were never in fact offered to Poland. "Herr von Ribbentrop's whole demeanour," our Ambassador recorded, "during an unpleasant interview, was aping Herr Hitler at his worst."

On September 1st, at dawn, the German troops invaded Poland. On the afternoon of that day Sir Neville Henderson was instructed to inform the German Government that unless they were prepared "to give His Majesty's Government satisfactory assurances that the German Government have suspended all aggressive action against Poland and are prepared promptly to withdraw their forces from Polish territory, His Majesty's Government in the United Kingdom will without hesitation fulfil their obligations to Poland." A similar communication was made by the French Ambassador. No reply was received from the German Government and the invasion of Poland, accompanied by intense aerial bombardment, continued unabated. By a telegram sent off from London at 5.0. a.m. on September 3rd, Sir Neville Henderson was instructed to inform the German Government that unless a satisfactory reply were received to his previous communication "not later than 11.0 a.m. British Summer Time to-day, September 3rd, a state of war will exist between the two countries as from that hour."

No such assurance was received.

5

At 11.15 on the morning of Sunday, September 3rd, Mr. Chamberlain informed the country by wireless that we were now at war. "You cannot imagine," he said, "what a bitter blow it is to me that all my long struggle to win peace has failed. Yet I cannot believe that there is anything more or anything different that I could have done, and that would have been more successful. Up to the very last it would have been quite possible to have arranged a peaceful and honourable settlement between Germany and Poland. But Hitler would not have it. . . . We have a clear conscience. We have done all that any country could do to establish peace, but a situation in which no word given by Germany's ruler could be trusted, and no people or country could feel themselves safe, had become intolerable. . . . Now may God bless you all and may He defend the right. For it is evil things that we shall be fighting against: brute force, bad faith, injustice, oppression and persecution."

Evil things.

CHAPTER IX

WHAT ARE THE REAL CAUSES?

ON Friday, October 6th, 1939, after he had seized Poland and occupied Warsaw, Herr Hitler, in a speech to the Reichstag, offered universal and eternal peace. He was prepared, it seems (apart from that little question of the colonies) to give Great Britain all that she had ever demanded. There would be a world peace conference, disarmament, the abolition of the bombing aeroplane, the open door for trade, and the reconstitution of the League of Nations. If England accepted these terms, then in truth the world would settle down to an era of unexampled peace and prosperity. If she rejected these terms, then upon her alone would fall the responsibility for the disasters which would follow. Mr. Chamberlain, in his lucid speech of October 12th, gave the only possible answer to this stratagem.

It was as if George Joseph Smith, having been convicted of the murder of Miss Mundy, Miss Burnhand and Miss Lofty, had addressed Mr. Justice Scrutton as follows: "It is no longer possible for you, my Lord, to restore life to either of these three ladies, since they are dead. It may be some comfort for you to know that I intend to preserve their ashes in an urn of my own special design. I now propose that you and I, my Lord, should regard the difference of opinion which has arisen between us in connection with these three brides as a thing of the past. I am prepared to offer you my hand here and now. I am prepared to go further. I am prepared to give my word of honour that henceforward I shall commit no further murders; that my next marriage (since all my previous brides are dead) will not be of a bigamous nature; and that never shall either I myself or any of my future brides enter a bath again. If you give me your hand on this, then our misunderstanding is over for ever. But if you insist, my Lord, upon the sentence which you have just passed, then the responsibility for the ensuing execution will rest upon your head alone."

There will be those who will protest as follows: "But this is an absurd and misleading analogy. We admit (since it amuses you to put it in that curious way) that Adolf Hitler has been found guilty before the tribunal of world-opinion of the murders of Austria, Czechoslovakia and Poland. We admit that he plotted these murders with deliberation and executed them with skill and cruelty. We admit even that you have exposed his methods and have shown how consistent has been his technique throughout. But when you end by comparing his case to that of George Smith when standing condemned by Mr. Justice Scrutton we can follow you no further. It was the business of Mr. Justice Scrutton to see to it that, once the jury had found Smith guilty of murder, he should be condemned to be hanged by the neck until he was dead. It is not our business to hang Adolf Hitler. We may deplore his conduct, but we have no need to exact retribution. There is a further difference between Mr. Justice Scrutton and ourselves. For whereas the policemen at the disposal of the court were sufficiently numerous to make it certain that Smith would be hanged with rapidity and ease, the execution of Adolf Hitler will entail agony for many millions of people. We see no reason, therefore, why this country or France should become involved in war merely because the ruler of Germany has broken his treaties and possessed himself of three countries in the East of Europe. What on earth, we ask you, has this to do with us? Why, therefore, have we gone to war?"

I propose, in this chapter, to answer that question.

2

The British people are by nature peaceful and kindly. They desire nothing on earth except to retain their liberties, to enjoy their pleasures, and to go about their business in a tranquil frame of mind. They have no ambition for honour and glory, and they regard wars, and even victories, as silly, ugly, wasteful things. They are not either warriors or heroes until they are forced to become so; they are sensible and gentle women and men.

In common with other branches of the Anglo-Saxon race they are a mixture of realism and idealism. Being somewhat indolent by temperament, it is only by dire necessity that they can be stirred to do unpleasant things. Yet when this necessity arises they like to make a virtue of it. This leads them at times to render unto God the things which are Cæsar's and has earned them the reputation of hypocrisy. In many ways, this reputation is unfair. No Englishman feels really happy unless both his practical and his moral instincts are engaged.

This sleepy, decent and most pacific race can only

be roused to violent action by two emotions: the first is fear; the second is anger.   Before he agrees to make war the Briton must have (a) a sense of personal danger and (b) a sense of personal outrage   His deep instinct of self-preservation, and his long moral tradition must simultaneously be aroused.   Ever since 1933 Adolf Hitler has titivated one or other of these two emotions but, until March 15th, 1939, he did not provoke them both simultaneously.   Until that vital date, half the people of Great Britain were frightened without being angry and the other half were angry without being frightened.   The combination of menace and humiliation which Herr Hitler contrived on March 15th united these two halves.

Let me begin with the menace, since it aroused our practical side, the instinct for self-preservation.   Why did the whole British people, on that March 15th, 1939, feel that the rape of Prague was a menace to our own existence?

During the previous six years the thought of "national security" had seldom been absent from our minds.   A sense of impending and imponderable danger hung over us night and day.   Each one of us responded to the acute discomfort of such anxiety in different ways.   Some tried to find ease of mind by dismissing the danger as imaginary and by repeating as some mystic incantation the formula: "There will be no war."   Others sought relief in believing that it might be possible for us to withdraw from the dangerous infections of Europe and to seek isolation in our Empire overseas.   Others again urged that the cancer was rapidly increasing and that only by early and drastic operation could it be removed.   While others believed in all sincerity that the menace

was not as malignant as some supposed and that by
a little patience, a little tact, a little conciliation the
wild animal which threatened us might be satisfied
and tamed.

It was this latter school of thought which produced
and directed the policy of appeasement. It is easy
to condemn that policy. It is all too easy to be wise
after the event and to contend that if we had risked
a little for the League of Nations in 1935 we should
not be risking our all to-day. It is easy to argue that
had we and France taken a strong line in 1936,
Germany would not have fortified the Rhineland and
thus provided herself with a barrier behind which she
could increase her power and her depredations in the
East. It is easy to condemn our Government for
not having intervened in Austria or Czechoslovakia,
for not having introduced conscription earlier, for
not having rushed in 1933 into a vast programme of
armament in the air. It is impossible to deny that
the Nazis have been able to delude and trick us at
every turn. It is impossible to deny that we were
too slow to realise the nature of their ambition or the
extreme cunning of their method. Their technique
has been, as I have tried to show, consistent
throughout.

I am conscious that as this story has been unfolded
the British Government have been made to seem
amazingly optimistic, gullible and blind. We must
remember, however, that at each stage Herr Hitler
knew exactly what he wanted, could guard his own
secrets, could operate with the utmost speed and
discipline, and was deterred by no considerations of
consistency or honour. The British Government
were throughout blinded by their fierce detestation
of war. Even had they realised earlier, that Herr

Hitler's ambition was unlimited and that he would never be satisfied with minor gains, they could not have taken preventive action without the approval of the British public. Until Herr Hitler made the gross error of tearing up the Munich agreement and thereby humiliating Great Britain in the person of her Prime Minister, such approval would not have been given.

It is easy also to criticise Mr. Chamberlain for the rigidity with which, until March 15th, 1939, he pursued a policy which has since been proved mistaken. Yet we must remember that throughout the period he was reflecting the ideas and wishes of a great mass, perhaps even a great majority, of British opinion. The Prime Minister is representative of those great civic virtues which have rendered our mercantile community the backbone of the country; he was throughout honourable, patient and sincere. By sacrificing so much in the cause of appeasement he may not perhaps have rendered peace more certain, but he assuredly showed the country and the world that war, if it came, would not be of our contrivance; that we should enter upon it with loathing but with resolution; and that our hands were clean.

3

What has all this to do with the instinct of self-preservation? It has this to do. The motive of self-preservation operated throughout the period from 1933–1939. Until March 15th last it was believed by the Prime Minister and his intimate advisers that if we could only avoid a head-on collision our own life might be preserved. After

March 15th they cherished no such illusions. The tiger was not merely attacking the native huts down in the village; he was fixing lustful eyes upon our own large bungalow. Hitler was out for loot. And since the British and French Empires offered the richest loot in the world, it was probable, it was even certain, that in the end we also should be attacked. It is this realisation which accounts for the sudden reversal of policy after March 15th. In a single night the British people found that their instinct of self-preservation had been aroused. It had been aroused, if I may repeat myself, by the realisation that Herr Hitler was not out to defend his own rights but to violate the rights of others. It was then at last that we saw that he was a menace to the world.

The British people have never been accustomed to formulate their instincts in logical terms. They possess the most sensitive antennæ, and when danger threatens these antennæ convey warnings to the whole ant-heap or hive. Such warning was conveyed on March 15th. For 250 years and more the British people have known instinctively that their safety depended upon preventing the continent of Europe and therefore their sea communications from falling under the domination of a single Power. It was this instinct which prompted them (at great cost to themselves) to fight Spain, Holland, Louis XIV, Napoleon and William II. They called this instinct by varying names. Sometimes they called it "The Balance of Power"; at other, and more sentimental moments, they called it "The protection of the smaller Nations." Yet whatever names they may have given to the instinct it was there as a durable, firm and recurrent element in their national destiny.

It is a sound biological instinct; it is the instinct of self-preservation.

It is conditioned by hard and inescapable facts. Great Britain is a small island containing a large population dependent for their food supplies upon imports from overseas. She is also a small island situated but twenty-five miles from the European peninsula, and connected with her vast Empire, and its sources of food and raw materials, by tenuous and exposed arteries of communication. She is thus one of the most vulnerable countries upon earth. If once these slim arteries were severed then she would lose her very life-blood. Germany might be invaded and conquered, but she would still remain Germany. France might be invaded and conquered and would still remain France. If once Great Britain lost control over her own communications, she would not only cease to be a Great Power, but would cease to be a Power at all. She would become a parasite living upon the good-will of other organisms. She would not only lose her authority, her riches and her possessions; she would also lose her independence. It is for this reason that, once any European Power arouses our instinct of self-preservation, we become unanimously alarmed. We know that any fight into which we enter is a fight for life. Herr Hitler (stupidly from his point of view) has managed to arouse this instinct.

"But why," you may ask, "should Germany's seizure of a distant city in Central Europe constitute a menace to the British Empire?" For this reason. Because he thereby disclosed that his true ambition was one of conquest. Until then he had always had some plausible excuse for his depredations. There was no excuse at all for the seizure of Prague. It

was conquest, naked and undisguised. There was
no reason why, if he seized Prague, he might not also
seize Copenhagen, Amsterdam, Brussels, Berne and
Stockholm. A tiger had been let loose on Europe
and the little countries were not strong enough to
resist. It was not because Prague had been seized,
or Danzig threatened, that we were alarmed: Miss
Mundy might just as well have been Miss Jones or
Miss Smith; what frightened us was that murder was
abroad. It was not so much Poland that we
guaranteed thereafter; it was our help in catching
the murderer.

The motive of self-preservation is not an unselfish
motive; it is a selfish motive. We knew that if these
murders continued, if the tiger remained at large, all
the small States of Europe might succumb to his
might and ambition. He would attain to such
gigantic power that even the British Fleet might be
unable to restrain him. German armies might reach
Istambul and push on to the very confines of India.
German submarines might be based in Rotterdam.
German air forces might be congregated twenty-five
miles from Dover. The danger was personal and
immediate. The beacons flared a warning.

There are many people in England who believe
that war is in itself such an evil thing that it would
be better to surrender without resisting. If we were
at war with a civilisation, such as that of the United
States, which is of a standard equal, if not superior,
to our own, I should not question that argument. I
should willingly see Great Britain revert to the
position of a smaller Power rather than sacrifice the
lives of her people. Yet we are not fighting against
a civilisation which is equal to our own. We are
fighting against a civilisation which is lower than

that which we, through centuries of trial and error, have ourselves been able to evolve. It is at this stage that the motive of fear, or self-preservation, shades off into the moral motive, which expresses itself in anger. Why should our lovely Christian code of honour surrender to this pagan brutality? Why should the fine culture of France be wrecked by barbarian invasion? It is to prevent such surrenders that we are prepared to fight.

Let me now consider the moral motive.

4

We must be careful to avoid self-righteousness. The main motive governing the actions of any country, or any animal, must be the motive of self-preservation. I contend however that the Anglo-Saxon race cannot be fired to the extremes of sacrifice and effort unless a moral motive is also present. We know that to-day we are fighting for our lives. We also want to know that we are fighting for something more important than our lives. We are certainly fighting for something more important.

Were it mere selfishness that directs our motives, would it be conceivable that a Government which represents the propertied classes of this country would embark on war? Whatever may be the outcome of this struggle we can be certain that the rich will lose. Herr von Ribbentrop has consistently assured his Führer that never will a Conservative Government make war for a principle, since their only principle is the maintenance of their own privileges and fortunes. Whatever happens, these will go. If the instinct of self-preservation were the sole guiding instinct, then the British propertied classes would have allowed Hitler to possess all the world provided he left them with their own incomes and privileges. Quite deliberately, knowing full well the consequences of their actions, they are prepared to sacrifice all their possessions rather than to allow this evil to triumph. Is this selfishness? Seldom has a whole class committed suicide in so great a cause.

This is a national, and not a class, struggle. Herr von Ribbentrop (as all those who take a low view of human nature) has proved to be wrong. But is it true, as the German say, that the whole nation is in fact guided solely by the instinct of self-preservation and has no higher aim in mind? It is completely untrue. We entered this war to defend ourselves. We shall continue to, to its most bitter end, in order to save humanity.

I am well aware that this assertion will bring a smile to many lips and, if read by the Führer, will cause him to scream with rage. I am not, I think, self-righteous upon the subject. We have often, as during the South African War, departed from these ideals. We have often pretended that we were pursuing moral or unselfish purposes when we were in fact pursuing predatory and selfish purposes. We have in this manner acquired a great Empire and a very general reputation for hypocrisy. Yet it could scarcely be denied that the conception of "decency" and "fairness" is a peculiarly Anglo-Saxon conception and that we have constantly endeavoured in our home and foreign policy to apply those conceptions to our conduct. We have not always succeeded; we have often failed; but assuredly we have tried.

I should ask those who regard this assertion as an

instance of British cant to consider the following proposition. From 1815 to 1914 Great Britain was the strongest Power in the world. Her command of the seas, her vast financial resources, enabled her to have the decisive voice in almost any dispute which might arise between other nations. She possessed this overwhelming power for almost a century. Of late years that power, owing to the invention of the bombing aeroplane and other causes, has declined. Yet is there a single small State in Europe that has not regretted our loss of power? Is there a single small State in Europe to-day who would not rejoice if, owing to some amazing invention, we were again to become the arbiter of world affairs? Conversely, is there a single State in Europe which welcomes the tremendous power which Germany has amassed, or which does not regard with terror the ruthless nihilism of the Nazi system? Surely this is a true, and even a moderate, statement? Surely it is true that if between 1815 and 1914 Germany had been possessed of similar supremacy, she would not have exercised it, as we exercised it, in such a manner as to identify her own predominance with the freedom and self-development of the smaller European peoples? And if this be true, then surely the conclusion is also true, namely that we do in fact endeavour to exercise power in a more humane and progressive manner than do the rulers of Germany. And that therefore what is all too vaguely known as "The Anglo-Saxon Ideal" does in fact represent for mankind something higher than the ideals of the rubber truncheon and the concentration camp. Assuredly, as Mr. Chamberlain has said, we are fighting evil things.

The evolution of the human race, from the savage

E*

to the civilised man, has been marked by certain stages of advancement. The Greeks discovered the beauty of the liberated mind; the Nazis deny that the mind of the individual should ever be free. The Romans established the rule of law and the sanctity of Treaties; the Nazis have only their own Nazi law and have violated every treaty which they have signed. Christ taught us the lessons of gentleness, of tolerance, of loving kindness; the Nazis deny Christ as a Jew and despise human charity as a decadent virtue. The age of chivalry taught us that we should not kick in the stomach those who are weaker than ourselves; Herr Hitler proclaims that the weak have "no right to live." The French eighteenth century evolved the elegance of taste and the balance of reason; Herr Hitler has reduced taste to the level of a cheap picture post-card and has declared reason to be the enemy of the State. We in England have evolved the conception of "decency" and "fairness"; the Nazis regard these conceptions as hypocritical and debased. "Remember," said Herr Hitler, when addressing school children recently, "Remember to be hard." Their little faces blinked obediently into an expression of brutality.

Are we aware even now of the actual cruelty of the Nazi system?

I do not wish to indulge in atrocity stories. Any German of intelligence and courage, any neutral resident in Germany, will tell you how the Nazi Gauleiters have taken the soul of that magnificent people in their hands and twisted it until it has assumed the crooked, tortured, combative shape of the swastika. We know how family life in Germany has been poisoned by fear and delation, and how the children are taught in their schools to betray their parents to the local Nazi leaders. We know how scholars and men of letters have been deprived of their posts and driven from their country solely because they refused to teach or tell the lies which Dr. Goebbels demanded. We know how the great Nazi machine has taken the boys of Germany and stamped them into uniform shapes as if they were but buttons in a factory. We know that the whole energy of the system has devised the slogan: "Hear nothing that we do not wish you to hear. See nothing that we do not wish you to see. Believe nothing that we do not wish you to believe. Think nothing that we do not wish you to think." We know that all those who do not bow the knee to Baal, such as Pastor Niemöller and Cardinal Faulhaber, are imprisoned or persecuted. We know that all gaiety and laughter has been hushed. We know that they have taught their people not to think.

Do we always remember and realise the actual physical side? I have met a man who was sent to a German concentration camp and thereafter released. He managed to escape into Switzerland and I saw him later in Paris. He was an elderly man of short stature and great girth. On arrival at the camp he was made to take off all his clothes and to creep on all fours around the room. The youths of the S.S. who were in control of the camp amused themselves by flicking with wet towels at his naked frame. They then told him to urinate into the mouth of an elderly Jew, who was also stripped naked. When he refused to do so, they were both flogged until they were unconscious. I did not believe this story at the time. Since then I have heard other stories which confirm it in every detail. I cannot conceive that, in any circumstances which could possibly arise, could

youths of my own race either wish, or be allowed by
their elders, to behave with such obscenity. Even
animals do not expose each other to such humiliations. We have all in our experience met boys who
are capable of sadistic cruelty. Yet never in the history of civilised man have such boys been told that
what they did was right.

"Yes," you will answer, "that is all very shocking
and painful, but what has it to do with us?"

It has this to do. If England surrenders, the
whole of Europe will surrender. Our responsibility
is magnificent and terrible. I should not be willing
to sacrifice my life or the lives of my sons for any
material victory. I shall willingly sacrifice everything I possess to prevent the victory of this foul
and ghoulish idea.

"Yes," you may murmur, "all that is very noble.
But will it profit the world if in seeking to destroy
Hitler we succeed only in destroying ourselves? Is
it not possible that the Führer, having now obtained
his Lebensraum in Poland, may this time be sincere
in his assurances and may rest in peace?"

It is possible, but it is not probable. The risk is
too great to take. For if indeed Herr Hitler were
allowed undisturbed to digest and organise the vast
territories that he has conquered; if he be allowed,
owing to our surrender, to dominate indirectly the
other small countries of Europe; then he will say to
us at his good pleasure: "I am anxious, as I have
always been anxious, to place the relations between
Germany and the British Empire upon a permanently peaceful basis. All I ask of you is that you
should hand over to me your African colonies and
the Malay States; that you should transfer to me
the sum of £500,000,000 in gold and foreign credits;

and that you should give me the *Hood*, the *Nelson*, and the *Rodney* in addition to naval tonnage equal to those ships which were surrendered at Scapa Flow."

We shall then not be in a position to refuse this request. We shall thereafter become a vassal State.

I conclude with a sentence written by one who was, in his time, a personal friend of Hitler and a high Nazi official, and who left his leader and his country in honourable disgust. "Hitler," writes Dr. Rauschning, "is not a man with whom a reasonable being concludes an agreement: He is a phenomenon which one slays or is slain by."

We shall not be slain.

CHAPTER X

WAR AIMS

How often does one hear the expression: "Oh, but war settles nothing!" This is a thoughtless phrase. All great civilisations have, in the end, perished owing to defeat in war. It was the victory of their opponents which put an end to the Babylonian, the Persian, the Carthaginian, the Roman, the Byzantine and the Napoleonic Empires. Were Hitler to win this war, he would "settle" the British Empire once and for all.

Yet (as always with phrases which gain popular credence) there is an element of truth concealed under this inaccurate slogan. It is not war which settles nothing; war may settle certain things for ever; it is a bad peace which settles nothing. We must see to it therefore that at the end of this war we do not make a bad peace. We must learn from past experience. "We must not," in Mr. Eden's phrase, "make the same mistake again."

The first thing to do, therefore, is to be clear in our own minds what exactly were the mistakes which we made in 1919. Much nonsense has been talked, both here and in Germany, about the Treaty of Versailles. The Germans pretend that we tricked them at the time of the armistice into accepting a dictated peace. There are many people in this country who, without having ever studied the question seriously, are under the impression that the

Paris Conference imposed by force what in fact were "Carthaginian terms." Such people attribute all our subsequent misfortunes to the malignity and folly of the Versailles negotiators. This is incorrect.

It is inaccurate as to the past, and unimaginative as to the future. For if indeed we fall into the habit of thinking that the negotiators of Versailles were guilty of ignorant viciousness, then we shall also fall into the habit of believing that "all will be right next time." We shall, next time, be kinder and wiser. It will not be so easy as all that; it will be a tremendous task to remould a world after it has been shattered to bits. The negotiators of the 1919 Peace Treaties imagined that they knew exactly what errors had been committed by those who negotiated the Vienna settlement of 1815. They believed that they were "kinder and wiser." They arrived in a mood of arrogant complacency. Let us approach the next Peace Conference knowing well that the human mind is a small instrument and the human heart a fallible organ. Let us approach it with modesty, caution and acute awareness of the difficulties which we shall have to face.

I am now going to impose upon my readers a tiresome disquisition upon the true errors of Versailles. I advise those who may be bored by this digression to skip at once to section 3.

The Treaty of Versailles was not, as some suppose, a vicious and revengeful Treaty in the sense that the Treaties which a victorious Germany imposed upon Russia and Rumania were vicious Treaties. The mistake made by the Paris negotiations was that they were never clear at the time what sort of peace they really wanted to make. They fell between two stools. I was myself a member of the British

Delegation in Paris and watched the thing happening with impatience and distress. I have recorded my experiences, and the lessons which I derived from that exhausting fiasco, in my book entitled *Peace-making*. It is supposed to be bad taste on the part of an author to mention in a subsequent book any previous work of his own. But as this *Penguin* must be short, and as the subject is of importance, I refer those who are interested in the errors of Versailles to the long and careful consideration which I gave to the problem in the book which (with execrable taste) I have mentioned above. Let me summarise as shortly as I can the conclusions which, both at the time and fifteen years afterwards, imposed themselves upon my judgment. They were as follows.

2

I contended that the Peace Conference which drafted the Treaties of Versailles, St. Germain, Trianon, Neuilly and Sèvres, suffered from certain definite "misfortunes" and committed certain definite "mistakes." Under the heading of "misfortunes" I tabulated those circumstances which (although inevitable in the conditions of the time), created an atmosphere in which a just and reasonable Treaty of Peace became impossible. Under the heading of "mistakes" I tabulated those errors of thought and feeling which might have been avoided, and the commission of which rendered the ensuing Treaties unhealthy from the day of their birth.

I defined the misfortunes as follows. The greatest of all our misfortunes at the Peace Conference of 1919 was that it came after a war which had been hotly contested, which had entailed enormous suffering, which aroused the worst passions of the human soul, and which culminated in a victory so overwhelming that the conquered enemy had practically ceased to exist. The second misfortune followed from the first. Public opinion in the victorious democracies was, in the first months of 1919, in an injured state of mind. Had the peace negotiations been in the hands of professional diplomatists, the resultant Treaties might have been wiser and more humane. It was essential, however, that after a combat of such gigantic proportions the various Powers should be represented by their political leaders. These leaders inevitably provoked, and could not ignore, political, or even party, feeling at home. Mr. Lloyd George had to cope with a khaki House of Commons, and a jingo Press, who insisted not only upon immediate demobilisation of our armies (which imposed harmful time-pressure upon the negotiators), but also upon "squeezing the orange until the pips squeaked." When in March, 1919, Mr. Lloyd George endeavoured to mitigate the severity of the Treaty, he received a telegram signed by a majority of the House of Commons, suggesting that he was "Pro-German" and insisting that "the Hun has got to pay." President Wilson was also hampered by opposition in the Senate and among large sections of American opinion, and failed disastrously either to educate or to conciliate that opposition. M. Clemenceau (who, as Mr. Lloyd George once said to me, was "a rude but reasonable man") was accused of weakness and yielding by his own jingoes. The Italian delegates were much hampered by their own extremists. The representatives of the new States which had emerged from the chaos would, had they taken a moderate standpoint, have been at once replaced by other politicians of more excessive ambitions.

A third misfortune was that President Wilson, who ought to have remained as the distant arbiter of the White House, decided himself to enter the diplomatic arena. He thereby lost the aloofness, the impassivity, and even the authority which he ought to have possessed. He lost touch with his own public opinion. And the fourth misfortune was the choice of Paris as the seat of the Conference. There, in that nerve-stricken capital, the demons of rumour, suspicion and resentment did their deadly work. The Conference was conducted in an atmosphere of angry and hysterical rush.

So much for the misfortunes. They were not realised at the time and some of them (even when they were realised) could not be avoided. The mistakes might have been avoided. The fundamental mistake was that no very clear programme had been laid down in advance. Two conflicting principles (which for convenience may be called the "American" and the "French" principle) were in conflict. The Americans believed that it might be possible, through the instrument of the League of Nations, to create a new order of international affairs. The French (and notably Marshal Foch) were under no such illusions. The Americans hoped to create a system under which disputes between nations could be settled by sweet reasonableness. The French contended that if the nations of the earth were really as reasonable as the Americans supposed, then there would have been no need for any war and no need for any Peace Treaty. They foresaw that the day would come when Germany, at

that moment torn by inner strife and stunned by
defeat, would revive. All that they asked for was
that an impassable barrier should be created between
Germany and Western Europe. They asked for the
Rhine. I now think that they were right. I did not
think so at the time.

Either of these two conflicting theories might have
given us a permanent peace if each had been applied
to its fullest extent. It is possible, and I now think
probable, that if the Rhine frontier had really been
given to France, Germany would thereafter have
been deprived of the physical possibility of commit-
ting any further acts of aggression. It is possible,
and I now think probable, that if the doctrine of
President Wilson had been applied in its entirety
Germany would not have had the moral temptation
to seek to upset the Versailles settlement. The fundamental error which was made was to compromise
between these two opposites. Either there should
have been a peace of force or a peace of justice. The
peace which emerged from the Paris Conference
was unjust enough to cause resentment, but not
forceful enough to render such resentment impotent.
Germany was neither conciliated nor suppressed.
She was wounded, but not slain. It took her fourteen
years and more to recover from her wounds.

Compared to this fundamental error, all other
mistakes made by the Paris negotiators are of slight
importance. It was a mistake, for instance, not to
realise that the need for demobilisation would create
a time-pressure such as no statesman could resist.
There should have been a Preliminary Treaty cover-
ing the main points and imposed upon Germany.
A year later a final Treaty should have been negotiated when passions had died down and when it was

possible to discuss the issues involved in a reasonable spirit. It was a mistake, also, to have made the Conference a session of the victorious Powers and not to have invited enemy as well as neutral countries to assist in the deliberations. It was a mistake to have inserted into the Treaties devices (such as the Mandates system) which were clearly hypocrital, and claims (such as those for reparation payments) which were manifestly absurd. And finally it was a mistake to have allowed resentment to figure so patently in many clauses, and to have introduced undignified and unfair stipulations, such as the War Guilt Clause and the clauses regarding the punishment of "war criminals."

What, therefore, are the lessons to be learnt from these errors and misfortunes? They can be tabulated as follows:

1. Before the negotiators enter any future Peace Conference they must be clear in advance what kind of new world it is that they wish to create.

2. They must draw a sharp distinction between the Preliminary Treaty which must be *imposed* upon the enemy and the Final Treaty which must be *negotiated* with the enemy. The Preliminary Treaty should deal only with the physical facts of the situation, such as the withdrawal of troops, the evacuation of territory, the surrender of arms, and the demobilisation of armies. The Final Treaty should deal with the future political and economic structure of the world. The Preliminary Treaty should be imposed and signed immediately after the armistice. The negotiations for the Final Treaty should not even begin before one year has elapsed since the conclusion of war. Admittedly such a delay will keep the world in suspense for some eighteen months;

this is an inevitable disadvantage; even prolonged uncertainty is preferable to decisions come to in a mood of hatred and without sufficient consideration and calm.

3. The Preliminary Treaty should be imposed by the victors upon the vanquished. It should be a *Diktat*. The Final Treaty should be something wholly different. The vanquished enemy should be represented and his views and suggestions should be given every consideration. Nor is this all. The Conference, or Congress, should be held, not in one of the beligerent capitals, but in the capital of a neutral State, preferably at Washington. The secretariat of the Conference should be composed of citizens of that neutral state.

4. Each Power represented at the Conference should have as their delegates the leaders both of the Government and of the Opposition parties. They should have attached to them, in the capacity of fellow delegates or assistants, men and women who are outside politics and whose knowledge and experience is such as to command the respect of their countrymen.

5. It should be announced at the outset that the Congress is expected to last for at least twelve months so that public impatience may not be unnecessarily aroused.

6. Full publicity should be given to the proceedings of the Congress.

Such suggestions concern procedure. They have little to do with our present war aims as such. Yet I am convinced by my own experience of the Paris Conference that a correct procedure is vital to a just peace. It was not the intentions of the Paris

negotiators which were at fault, it was the methods
by which they sought to put these intentions into
practice. If we repeat the hurried, confused, hysterical and ill-considered procedure of 1919, we
shall assuredly end (however noble may be our feelings and intentions) in concluding a Peace which
shall be equally unsatisfactory to all concerned. It
is for this reason that I have placed correct procedure
in the very forefront of my examination of our
eventual terms of peace. I know that in so doing
I have seemed to go off on a tangent: it is not a
tangent.

3

The British people at the present moment are dis-
heartened by the fact that they do not know what
they are fighting for. The old slogan of "Make the
world safe for democracy" awakes no response whatsoever in their hearts. The cry of "Down with
Hitler" does not appeal to any sensible person as an
objective for which it is worth sacrificing the lives
of many men. We may feel deeply sorry for
Austria, Czechoslovakia and Poland, yet we do not
see why the whole future of the British Empire
should be imperilled for their advantage. We may
loathe the Nazi system from the very depths of our
souls, yet it is a hard thought that we must ourselves
adopt Nazi methods in order to defeat the thing that
we dislike.

The time will come, of course (and it will come
with thunder and fire), when the British people will
realise that they are fighting for their very existence.
It will suddenly be borne in upon them that all this
intricate discussion of Sudeten Germans and

corridors is a discussion, not of the disease itself, but of the symptoms of the disease. They will come to understand that unless we shoulder this relentless burden the whole of Europe will fall under Nazi domination and that not only will our own possessions and liberties be sacrificed, but that our actual independence will be lost. They will then know that this disaster is our opportunity.

I do not think that the great mass of our public as yet understand the true proportions of the issue. How could they? They have not been informed. The Government fluctuate between a realism which they refuse to admit and an idealism which is not believed in. The realism is this: "The British Empire is in grave danger of extinction." The idealism is this: "If we can avoid being defeated we shall save the world."

For even when our deep instinct for self-preservation is violently aroused, the British people will demand something more. They are unwilling to sacrifice the lives of their sons and lovers solely for material ends; when sorrow comes to them it will be for spiritual comfort that they will yearn. They will want to be certain that they are making these sad sacrifices, not for their own sakes, not even for the sake of their own children, but for the sake of future generations and for the sake of mankind as a whole.

It is no use trying to respond to this inarticulate feeling by drawing imaginary pictures of a "land fit for heroes to live in" or by painting vague landscapes of the shape of things to come. People are sick to death of these misty and sentimental generalisations. They may feel disgusted with Herr Hitler and they may ardently desire his discomfiture and fall. They may feel humiliated by the impotence which we have shown either to prevent or to control his depredations.   Their pride may be outraged and their honour besmirched.   They may dream vaguely that out of all this misery some better world may emerge.   Yet what they desire above everything is that their realism and their idealism should be united in a concrete programme; they want to know that we are fighting, not merely to defend our liberties, not merely to defeat an evil system, but to create a world in which these things shall not happen again. It is useless to tell them that these are in fact the very purposes for which a most unwilling Government has decided we must fight; they want to know *how*, when victory comes (and it will be a hard-won victory) this better world will be created.

They are tired of phrases and uplift; they want facts.   What are the facts?

All are to-day agreed that we cannot make peace so long as Herr Hitler and his gang remain the directors of Germany.   All are agreed that Germany must restore to Poland and Czechoslovakia the lands and liberties which she has filched.   All are agreed that the Austrian people must be given an absolutely free opportunity to declare their own wishes.   In order to achieve these aims we have no need to defeat Germany as we defeated her in 1918; all that we need is to prevent Germany from defeating us.   Yet if Germany is to see reason in time it is essential that the German people should realise what sort of peace-terms we have in mind.   The British Government may be right in refusing to formulate detailed peace-terms at a time when the duration and nature of the war is uncertain.   But if they cannot say what they *do* mean to do, they can certainly say what they do *not* mean to do.   They should announce at once that from this war we, for our own part, desire not one inch of anybody else's territory. That we have no desire whatsoever to ruin the German people either economically or politically. That all we desire is to put an end to this system of violence and to fashion a new European system in which all peaceful countries shall have an equitable and creative share.

It must be remembered that we defeated German militarism in 1918; it emerged from its own ashes. It must be remembered that in 1919 we created what we hoped would be a new world-order in the shape of the League of Nations; it collapsed under the first strain. Is it possible to define our present war aims in such a manner as will convince reasonable men and women in Great Britain and Germany that after this great darkness will come a radiant dawn?

I am not an optimist. I do not believe in radiant dawns. But I do believe that if we in Great Britain are resolute and wise there will emerge from this catastrophe something which may well give hope to the world.

4

Let me approach the problem in a practical manner. There are in fact two problems. The first is the problem of Germany as expressed in the question: "How can you permanently control a nation of 80,000,000 situated in the very centre of Europe?" The second is the problem of the future world-order as expressed in the question: "Now that the League of Nations has failed, what other similar organisation could you put in its place?"

I admit that the German problem is almost insoluble. There are those who believe that, with the fall of Hitler, we might be able to create a new

Germany centred upon Vienna and reverting
gradually to a loose Germanic federation, analagous
to the "dear little Germanies"of before 1871. Under
this theory that admirable young man, the Arch
Duke Otto, would be restored to the throne of his
fathers and be nominated German Emperor. Everything would be done to minister to the happiness and
prosperity of this new Austrian Empire. A Danubian
federation would be created in the East bound to
Vienna by a customs and monetary union. Large
loans would be accorded to the new State such as
would wipe out all indebtedness and set the economic
machine in working order. Vienna, under such a
system, would become both the Paris and the London
of Central and Eastern Europe. The German people
(who have never cared for the drab ugliness of Berlin)
would be entranced by this revival of former elegance.
Their sense of inferiority would vanish; their latent
hatred of the Prussian would revive; the "Blue
Danube " would succeed the "Wacht am Rhein."
Simultaneously all the smaller dynasties would be
restored. There would be kings again in Saxony
and Bavaria, in Wurtemberg and Hanover. Herzogs
and Erzherzogs would abound. And as a punishment, the Prussians would be obliged to preserve the
Nazi system in Berlin and Königsberg for a period
of twenty-five years.

I fear that this attractive theory is not sensible. In
the first place, the conception of a single Germany
has now taken a firm hold upon the consciousness of
the modern German generation. The old regional
patriotism, the old loathing of Berlin, is dying out.
The decentralisation of Germany would not be
popular with the Germans themselves. In the
second place, we must face the fact that once the

Nazis disappear the communists will come in. It may well be that Herr Hitler will himself introduce a brand of National-Bolshevism before he disappears. But it is certain that once the façade of the Nazi system begins to crack the whole structure will collapse in a vast heap of rubble carrying with it all the traditions and the memories out of which the older Germany could be rebuilt. It will be a sad, if necessary, day for humanity when that disaster occurs. No mercy will be shown by the German proletariat to the little party bosses, the small Gauleiters, who have bullied and robbed them all these years. It may well be, as I have suggested, that the Führer, foreseeing this eventuality, may himself lead the communist movement and himself conduct the purge of all the Nazi officials. That will be a strange and blood-stained spectacle.

I do not, for these reasons, believe that it would be possible after a disastrous war, to recreate the old rococo Germany of the eighteenth century. I do not believe, however, that once the spell is broken, once the Hitler legend is smashed, the German people will emerge from the cataleptic trance in which he has held them. There may follow a period of internal disorder accompanied by appalling massacres and wide starvation. After that period the German people will not, for thirty years at least, desire again to try to rule the world by force. Provided that the peace terms imposed upon them are not such as to outrage their pride or to drive them to desperation the world will have thirty years in which to create a new world-order which shall be so powerful that even Germany will not dare to defy it; and so just that even the Germans will not feel aggrieved.

5

How is that world-order to be created? The
League of Nations was an admirable institution but
it had two grave defects. In the first place, it did
not possess armed forces such as could enable it to
impose its own decisions upon a recalcitrant member.
In the second place, none of the member States
made any sacrifice of their national sovereignty.
But for these two defects (and they were fundamental)
the League might well have achieved the pacification
of the world.

Let me examine in greater detail how these two
defects might now be remedied. The last time we
attempted the probable: this time we must surmount
the impossible. I am well aware that the difficulties
in the way of providing the League of Nations with a
force of its own are almost insurmountable: they
have got to be surmounted. It is evident that such
a force, if it is to be absolutely effective, must be more
powerful than any force which might be arrayed
against it. It must be more powerful, for instance,
than the combined forces of Germany, Russia, Italy
and Japan. To maintain, equip and train so vast an
international army would clearly be beyond the
bounds of sense. Is there no other way by which
the League could be rendered dominant? I think
there is. In the first place, under a general armament agreement, the forces of each State would be
reduced to the size required by their own internal
needs. Germany, for instance, would be allowed a
larger army than Great Britain and Great Britain be
allowed a larger navy than Germany. It should not

be beyond the bounds of human common-sense to
agree upon these quota figures. Such reduction
would, of course, not give the member States that
sense of absolute security which alone would induce
them to entrust their defences to an organisation outside their own control. Something more would be
needed. The air weapon provides the "something
more." It could be laid down that no country in
Europe should be allowed to possess any aeroplanes
at all, whether civil or military. The only institution
permitted to possess aeroplanes would be the League
of Nations. On the civil side, great international
air routes would be operated by the League as a
general utility undertaking. The League would also
possess a highly trained fighting air force with pilots
drawn only from the smaller countries. By this
means ruthless and immediate punishment (and there
would have to be no false sentimentality on this
point) could be administered to any State which,
after submitting its case to League arbitration, either
refused to accept the award or started aggressive
action against any of its neighbours.

Consider, for instance, what would have been the
development of the German-Polish dispute had such
a system existed. Germany and Poland would each
have been summoned to the League Court and told
to state their case. The Court might well have
decided that the corridor should remain Polish,
whereas Danzig should go to Germany under special
guarantees ensuring Poland's use of the waterway
and harbours. Supposing that Poland had refused
to evacuate Danzig, then Warsaw would have been
relentlessly bombed by League aeroplanes. Supposing that Germany had refused to abide by the
award and had invaded the corridor, then Berlin in

its turn would have suffered terrific punishment.
The decisions of the League Court would not have
been violated again.

Let us not imagine, however, that such a system
would be easy to create. It would require imagina-
tion and unselfishness on the part of Great and Small
Powers alike. The whole thinking power of the
United States would have to be devoted to this
problem. Above all, the scheme would be unwork-
able unless every single European Power participated.
It would be little use, for instance, for the League to
possess 2,000 bombing aeroplanes if the U.S.S.R.
refused to join in the scheme and retained 3,000
bombing aeroplanes of her own. All European
Powers would have to be forced, probably by
measures of joint blockade, to enter into this mutual
insurance. That would be a difficult and dangerous
phase in the whole plan.

Force, moreover, would not be enough. The new
League would also have to offer its members great
advantages. That brings me to the second main
defect in the present League of Nations, namely the
refusal of member States to sacrifice their sovereignty.
What do I mean by that?

There was a time when England was divided into
seven separate States, each passionately jealous of its
own rights and privileges. England only became a
peaceful and a progressive Power when these seven
States fused into one. Each of them surrendered
something for the good of the whole. I am convinced that Europe will only become a peaceful and
a prosperous continent if each of the present Nation
States surrender something of their independence for
the good of the whole. We must, in other words,
create something far wider and higher than the old

League of Nations; we must create the United States of Europe.

What sacrifices will this entail? Let us assume that such a European federation were created. We should find that the interests of each member of the federation fell into three general categories. There would be local interests; public utility undertakings; and federal interests. By local interests I mean housing, unemployment, social services, education and so on. By public utility undertakings I mean international transit, airways, posts and telegraphs, broadcasting and so on. By federal interests I mean the vast problems of international finance and commerce, the direction of foreign policy, and the control of armaments. If the United States of Europe were created we should continue to manage our local interests in our own manner and through our own Parliament. Public utility undertakings would, without damage to ourselves, be organised upon a European rather than upon a national basis. But we should agree that the extent and nature of our armaments, the general lines of our foreign policy, and the use of our raw materials and credits should conform to general lines laid down by the Central Federal Authority of the United States of Europe.

Would that in fact be so terrible a sacrifice? Would the man or woman at Leicester or in Maidstone really suffer loss of pride or property if the rubber of the Malay States or the copper in Rhodesia were placed in some common pool for the benefit of all nations? Would it really mean for us a loss of prestige or power if all our African colonies were placed under the mandatory system and administered in the interests of the natives and of humanity as a whole? That in fact is the system which we are already adopting. We should notice little change.

And in return for this we should achieve a world which is worth fighting for. A world without conceit or cruelty, without greed and lies. If Hitler triumphs, then such a world will be impossible for many generations. It is Britain alone that can create the United States of Europe.

Did I believe that this war were no more than a ghastly episode provoked by the unstable vanity of a single man, then indeed I should surrender to despair, knowing that the ensuing peace would also be no more than an episode. It is because I am convinced that this war, as it develops, will assume gigantic proportions that I believe that the final settlement will also be gigantic. Because of that faith I face the future with sorrow, with resolution, but without fear.

ANTONY BEEVOR

D-DAY: THE BATTLE FOR NORMANDY

'A knockout reassessment of one of the Second World War's great set-piece battles. Swoops from the vicious close-quarter fighting in the hedgerows to the petrified French onlookers and onwards to the political leaders wrestling with monumental decisions' *Sunday Times*

'Beevor has succeeded brilliantly. *D-Day* can sit proudly alongside his other masterworks on Stalingrad and the fall of Berlin. Superbly brings the events of that summer to life again' Patrick Bishop, *Daily Telegraph*

'As near as possible to experiencing what it was like to be there . . . It is almost impossible for a reader not to get caught up in the excitement' Giles Foden, *Guardian*

'A magnificent portrait of the horrors, splendours and absurdities of the greatest campaign of the western war. A master of the art of casting brilliant new illumination upon familiar themes . . . Beevor has assembled a mass of unfamiliar sources, fresh voices, and untold anecdotes to create a saga as impressive as *Stalingrad* and *Berlin*. As powerful and authoritative an account of the battle for Normandy as we are likely to get. A worthy memorial' Max Hastings, *Sunday Times*

'*D-Day* is a triumph of research . . . on almost every page there's some little detail that sticks in the mind or tweaks the heart. This is a terrific, inspiring, heartbreaking book' Sam Leith, *Daily Mail*

ANTONY BEEVOR

STALINGRAD

The classic international bestseller recounting the epic turning point of the Second World War.

'The colossal scale of Stalingrad, the megalomania, the utter absurdity, the sheer magnitude of the carnage, are marvellously captured in Beevor's history' Richard Bernstein, *The New York Times*

'This superb work of narrative history (all of human despair, and also of heroism is there) chilled the marrow of my bones' Antonia Fraser, *Sunday Times*

'Magnificent' John Keegan, *Daily Telegraph*

'Brilliant' *The Times*

'A magnificent winter tapestry . . . reads like a novel rather than the superb history book it really is' *Daily Telegraph*

'Superb . . . a compelling tale of human tribulation' Max Hastings

ANTONY BEEVOR

BERLIN: THE DOWNFALL 1945

'Fascinating, extraordinary, gripping' Jeremy Paxman

'Recounts, in harrowing detail and with formidable skill, the brutal death throes of Hitler's Reich at the hands of the rampaging Red Army' Boyd Tonkin, *Independent*

'Makes us feel the chaos and the fear as if every drop of blood was our own . . . compellingly readable, deeply researched and beautifully written' Simon Sebag Montefiore, *Spectator*

'An irresistibly compelling narrative of events so terrible that they still have the power to provoke wonder and awe' Adam Sisman, *Observer*

'A masterpiece' Michael Burleigh, *Guardian*

HUGH SEBAG-MONTEFIORE

DUNKIRK: FIGHT TO THE LAST MAN

'A narrative triumph. I have not read a better account' Max Hastings, *Sunday Telegraph*

The dramatic rescue in May 1940 of British troops fleeing from the Nazi war machine at Dunkirk was not just about what happened at seas and on the beaches: the evacuation would never have succeeded had it not been for the tenacity of the British soldiers who stayed behind to fight on so that the rest of the Army could be saved.

Outnumbered and outgunned by the advancing panzers, these brave young men stood their ground, combining a dogged determination to do their duty with occasional acts of spectacular heroism. Although they and their officers rightly concluded that some German units would be taking no prisoners, they were instructed not to give way until they had fired their last bullets, they were to fight to the last man.

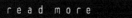

PENGUIN WORLD WAR II COLLECTION

FIRST LIGHT
GEOFFREY WELLUM

Two months before the outbreak of the Second World War, seventeen-year-old Geoffrey Wellum becomes a fighter pilot with the RAF . . .

Desperate to get in the air, he makes it through basic training to become the youngest Spitfire pilot in the prestigious 92 Squadron. Thrust into combat almost immediately, Wellum finds himself flying several sorties a day, caught up in terrifying dogfights with German Me 109s.

Over the coming months he and his fellow pilots play a crucial role in the Battle of Britain. But of the friends that take to the air alongside Wellum many never return.

PENGUIN WORLD WAR II COLLECTION

THE CRUEL SEA
NICHOLAS MONSARRAT

Based on the author's own vivid experiences, *The Cruel Sea* is the nail-biting story of the crew of HMS *Compass Rose*, a corvette assigned to protect convoys in World War Two.

Darting back and forth across the icy North Atlantic, *Compass Rose* played a deadly cat and mouse game with packs of German U-boats lying in wait beneath the ocean waves.

Packed with tension and vivid descriptions of agonizing U-boat hunts, this tale of the most bitter and chilling campaign of the war tells of ordinary, heroic men who had to face a brutal menace which would strike without warning from the deep . . .

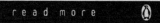
PENGUIN WORLD WAR II COLLECTION

TUMULT IN THE CLOUDS
JAMES GOODSON

Anglo-American James Goodson's war began on Sept 3rd 1939, when the *SS Athenia* was torpedoed and sank off the Hebrides. Surviving the sinking and distinguishing himself rescuing survivors, Goodson immediately signed on with the RAF. He was an American, but he wanted to fight.

Goodson flew Spitfires for the RAF before later joining his countrymen with the Fourth Fighter Group to get behind the controls of Thunderbolts and Mustangs where he became known as 'King of the Strafers'.

Chock full of breathtaking descriptions of aerial dogfights as well as the stories of others of the heroic 'few', *Tumult in the Clouds* is the ultimate story of War in the air, told by the one of the Second World War's outstanding fighter pilots.

PENGUIN WORLD WAR II COLLECTION

PANZER LEADER
HEINZ GUDERIAN

Heinz Guderian – master of the Blitzkrieg and father of modern tank warfare – commanded the German XIX Army Corps as it rampaged across Poland in 1939.

Personally leading the devastating attack which traversed the Ardennes Forest and broke through French lines, he was at the forefront of the race to the Channel coast. Only Hitler's personal command to halt prevented Guderian's tanks and troops turning Dunkirk into an Allied bloodbath.

Later commanding Panzergruppe 2 in Operation Barbarossa, Guderian's armoured spearhead took Smolensk after fierce fighting and was poised to launch the final assault on Moscow when he was ordered south to Kiev. In the battle that followed, he helped encircle and capture over 600,000 Soviet troops after days of combat in the most terrible conditions.

Panzer Leader is a searing firsthand account of the most effective fighting force in modern history by the man who commanded it.

PENGUIN WORLD WAR II COLLECTION

THE NEXT MOON
ANDRE HUE & EWEN SOUTHBY-TAILYOUR

Andre Hue was a daredevil. By the age of twenty the Anglo-Frenchman had survived shipwreck and years undercover in France, sabotaging German supply lines. Returning to Britain, he was recruited by SOE to parachute behind enemy lines on 5 June 1944, to unite resistance forces in Brittany and paralyse local German troops during the Allied invasion.

Though Hue's mission was fraught with difficulty – he missed his landing site, his secret base camp became the site of a pitch battle and a band of Cossacks tried to hunt him down – he knew that thousands of lives depended on his success or failure . . .

PENGUIN WORLD WAR II COLLECTION

EASTERN APPROACHES
FITZROY MACLEAN

Fitztroy Maclean was one of the real-life inspirations for super-spy James Bond. After adventures in Soviet Russia before the war, Maclean fought with the SAS in North Africa in 1942. There he specialised in hair-raising commando raids behind enemy lines, including the daring and outrageous kidnapping of the German Consul in Axis-controlled Iraq.

Maclean's extraordinary adventures in the Western Desert and later fighting alongside Tito's partisans in Yugoslavia are blistering reading and show what it took to be a British hero who broke the mould . . .